SHORT WALKS FROM

Cheshire
Pubs

James F. Edwards

COUNTRYSIDE BOOKS
NEWBURY, BERKSHIRE

First Published 1996
© James F. Edwards 1996

COUNTRYSIDE BOOKS
3 Catherine Road
Newbury, Berkshire

ISBN 1 85306 395 9

*This book is dedicated to the Rehabilitation Engineering staff
at the Disablement Services Centre, Withington, Manchester, whose
hard work brings solace to less fortunate members of society.*

Designed by Mon Mohan
Cover illustration by Colin Doggett
Photographs and Maps by the author

Produced through MRM Associates Ltd., Reading
Typeset by The Midlands Book Typesetting Company, Loughborough
Printed by Woolnough Bookbinding, Irthlingborough

Contents

Area map showing locations of the walks.

Publisher's Note

We hope that you obtain considerable enjoyment from this book; great care has been taken in its preparation. However, changes of landlord and actual closures are sadly not uncommon. Likewise, although at the time of publication all routes followed public rights of way or permitted paths, diversion orders can be made and permissions withdrawn.

We cannot of course be held responsible for such diversion orders and any inaccuracies in the text which result from these or any other changes to the routes nor any damage which might result from walkers trespassing on private property. However, we are anxious that all details covering the walks and the pubs are kept up to date and would therefore welcome information from readers which would be relevant to future editions.

Introduction

Designed very much with families in mind, each walk in this book commences at an appealing inn, passes through attractive scenery and provides an opportunity to visit places of interest, such as historic houses, parks and gardens, potteries, water mills, museums, ice cream farms and visitor centres.

The time span covered by the attractions goes from the Roman remains at Chester, medieval Norton Priory, the splendid halls of Arley, Tatton, Gawsworth and Little Moreton, the Industrial Revolution at Quarry Bank Mill, the 20th-century motor museum at Mouldsworth to the futuristic fascination of Jodrell Bank where the wonders of the universe unfold.

An entrance charge is payable for many of the attractions but of course, you do not have to visit them, as each walk is enjoyable in its own right. However, it is recommended that they are not omitted because you learn so much about the county and its history by visiting them.

Times when food is available have been indicated in the individual pub descriptions. General pub opening times have not been included due to the fact that they are often changed. However, these can always be obtained by using the telephone number which is given at the end of each description. Also, where the menu is the subject of constant variation, only an outline of the type of food available is given. Again each pub can be contacted in order to obtain specific menu details.

Furthermore, it must be stressed that parking is only for patrons. Alternative parking locations, when available, have been indicated in the text.

What you put on your feet is important. Waterproof walking shoes or boots are recommended, preferably worn over woollen socks. Smooth-soled shoes should not be worn as they can cause accidents and make walking hard work, especially after wet weather. Lightweight waterproof clothing should always be carried to combat the variable English weather. A small rucksack can be useful for carrying such items as food, cameras, binoculars and the like, which help to make a walk that much more enjoyable. It is also recommended that when a visit to a country house is undertaken a change of footwear is carried as muddy boots are not appreciated in such places.

A prime objective has been to provide direct, no-nonsense route descriptions for each walk, coupled with a clear accompanying sketch map. For those requiring more detail, the relevant OS Landranger 1:50 000 map numbers are given.

Do not be afraid to venture out during the winter months, for an excursion on a cold, clear day when frost has hardened the ground underfoot can be most rewarding, especially when coupled with a warming drink and a hearty meal taken in pleasant surroundings. However, if you wish to enjoy the facilities of an inn following the completion of a walk please remember to leave muddy walking boots in your car.

Finally, some words of thanks. As with previous surveys I have been accompanied during the preparations for this book by my mother and Jackie Ridgway, both of whom have made valued contributions to the finished work. Tim Birtles, Head Ranger of Tatton Estate gave freely of his time. An enjoyable afternoon was spent with James Peacop, who runs the Mouldsworth Motor Museum and is fascinated, as is the author, by all kinds of motorised transport. Special thanks go to Mrs Sealey of Somerset Lodge, Cholmondeley Castle Estate, for providing much useful background information. The task of deciphering my handwriting and converting it into a typed manuscript was expertly carried out by Kath Mannion. I must also thank all the managers and landlords of the various inns for taking time out from their busy schedules in order to provide answers to my many questions.

James F. Edwards
Spring 1996

1 Wilmslow
The Boddington Arms

Modern day Wilmslow is an attractive town which straddles the valleys formed by the rivers Bollin and Dean. This close proximity to abundant supplies of water acted as a catalyst for 18th and 19th-century mill owners who developed silk and cotton mills in the area. Although most of these mills have now disappeared, one of the largest, Quarry Bank Mill, has survived to become an award winning museum where the modern day visitor can gain some impressions of a working way of life long since gone.

Situated on the outskirts of Wilmslow, the Boddington Arms is a large establishment with a bright interior where a wide choice of food and drink can be consumed in comfort.

Drink from the bar includes draught bitter beers from Boddingtons and Higsons, Murphy's Irish Stout, mild beers, lagers from Stella Artois and Heineken, and Strongbow cider. There is also a superb selection of spirits and liqueurs, together with a comprehensive range of wines. Minerals, fresh fruit juices and other soft drinks are also on offer. The choice of food is so wide that the menu runs to nine pages of delicious offerings. There are assorted starters, steaks and grills, salad platters, chicken and fish, and three different set menus from 'The Special Table', all at very competitive prices. A tempting array of puddings, desserts and ice cream sundaes is also available. The inn welcomes families, and youngsters are well catered for with their own menu. At certain times, children under ten years of age can eat a free two course meal when accompanied by an adult diner.

Food can be obtained at the inn on Monday to Friday from 12 noon to 2.30 pm and 5.30 pm to 10.30 pm. On Saturday and Sunday food is served from 12 noon to 10.30 pm and 12 noon to 10 pm respectively. It is worth noting that the management requests that visitors are dressed 'smart casual', therefore it is probably best to sample the offerings of the inn prior to 'putting on the boots'. During the summer months trestle tables and benches are available for use in front of the pub.

Telephone: 01625 525849.

How to get there: The north-east Cheshire town of Wilmslow straddles the A34 to the south of the conurbation of Greater Manchester. At the centre of the town the A538 cuts across the A34 on its route between Prestbury and Altrincham. The Boddington Arms is just under one mile along the A538 from the centre of Wilmslow, in the direction of Altrincham.

Parking: There is a large car park at the inn. Alternatively, there are parking facilities at Quarry Bank Mill, to the south of the village of Styal, (follow the signs from Wilmslow town centre).

Length of the walk: 3½ miles. Map: OS Landranger 109 Manchester (inn GR 833814).

This walk combines some splendid scenery with a visit to the award-winning museum at Quarry Bank Mill, where a 200 year old working environment has been recreated. The outward journey takes you into the Bollin valley where the mill sits beside the river. The return leg meanders along wooded paths before returning to the outskirts of Wilmslow.

The Walk

On leaving the main entrance of the Boddington Arms, cross the facing car park and turn left to follow a roadside pavement alongside the A538. Pass King's Road and Greaves Road to continue along the roadside pavement. On passing a large car showroom, turn left to enter Mobberley Road. After 120 metres, and opposite a bungalow called Sandiway, leave the lane to the right where a footpath sign indicates 'Morley Green'.

The footpath hugs a hedgerow on the right and leads to a stile. Cross the stile to follow a hedged-in track. Keep forward over a crossing track

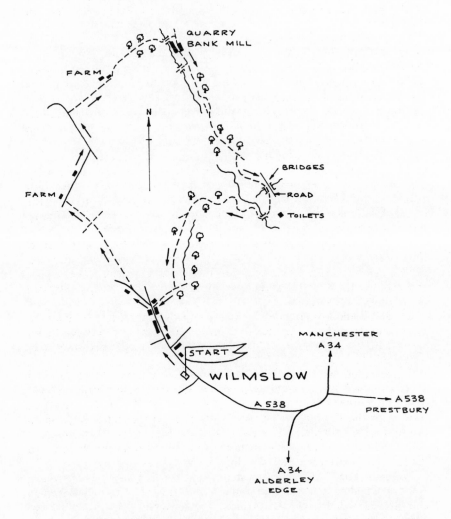

and arrive on a crossing lane opposite Moss Grove Farm. Turn right and follow the lane. Pass Nans Moss Farm and continue to a crossing road. Cross the road, turn left, and follow the roadside verge. After 200 metres, leave the road to the right where a footpath sign points along a farm approach drive. Go through a facing gate and continue towards farm buildings which can be seen straight ahead. Keep to the right of outbuildings to pass through a gate. On reaching the end of the outbuildings, bear diagonally left, and after a few metres join a grassy track where there is a fence on the left and trees and hedges on the right.

A stile by a facing gate takes you onto a rough, fenced-in track, which descends through trees. At the bottom of the descent bear left and then cross the Bollin via a bridge. On the right here, and adjacent to the river, can be seen the main building of Quarry Bank Mill. Continue past its gable end along a cobbled way and then turn right. In front of the mill building an inscription above a doorway tells you that the mill was built by Samuel Greg in 1784. A few more strides take you to the main entrance, where there is a reception area and shop.

The fascinating story of the mill has been brought to life through a series of exciting reconstructions and hands-on displays. Initially, only the spinning of yarn was carried out and, by the end of the 19th century, the output of yarn exceeded that of any other mill in the country. Weaving was then gradually introduced and by 1894 Quarry Bank's output was geared solely to this form of production.

There is so much to see at both the mill and the Apprentice House. Observe how the Gregs and their workforce coped with everyday life, cast an eye over the mill's water wheel – a 50 ton monster, 24 ft high – and explore the Waterforce Gallery which shows how water power can be harnessed and controlled.

Quarry Bank Mill is open to visitors throughout the year between 11 am and 6 pm (last admission 4.30 pm) in summer, and between 11 am and 5 pm (last admission 3.30 pm) from October to the end of March. Telephone for information: 01625 527468.

On completion of your visit, leave the main entrance, turn left and cross a cobbled yard. Ascend steps at the side of a display board relating to Styal Country Park and continue along a well-defined path. Ignore a turning to the right, where a path leads to a bridge and keep forward through tall Scots pines. The river can be seen on the right here. The path gradually climbs and then takes you along level terrain. Over to the left can be seen the exposed cliff face of a disused stone quarry.

The path goes close to the water's edge and is fenced on the right. A stout wooden footbridge traverses a small ravine. The path descends and merges with another path which joins from the right. Keep left and forward here to continue along a level stretch of path through trees, where there is an embankment on the left.

A little further on, the path forks, where there is a small boulder half buried in the ground. Take the right fork here, to follow a well-defined path that takes you close to the river, which is on your immediate right. The path leads to a footbridge at the side of a road bridge (1878). Immediately on crossing this footbridge you have entered a grassy

Quarry Bank Mill.

common, at the far side of which can be seen a single-storey brick building (which is in fact a toilet block adjacent to Twinnies Bridge car park). Bear right now and, after a few metres, enter a path which takes you through undergrowth. Cross a footbridge to traverse the river and turn right to follow a riverside path.

Ascend steps and follow the path as it skirts around the edge of Wilmslow Rugby Club. Descend steps and continue along the riverside. The marshy ground in this area has been traversed by boarding which quickly turns to the left. A combination of path and boarding leads to a facing climb up widely spaced steps through the trees. At the top of the climb the path forks. Keep left and ahead now, to pass over two wooden bridges. A great deal of work has been carried out on the path, as is evident from the boarding and fences which have been installed. The path follows the edge of a wooded valley, which slopes down to a stream on the left. After $1/4$ mile, arrive at a T-junction of paths. The path to the left goes to King's Road, but turn right here – where a sign indicates 'Altrincham Road'. Emerge from the path at a facing track which takes you between cottages and leads to a crossing road.

Cross the road and turn left to follow the roadside pavement. You are now back on part of your initial route. Continue, shortly to arrive back at the Boddington Arms and the car.

2 Halton Gate
The Barge

The village of Halton and nearby Halton Gate have, despite much development in the area, managed to retain their identities. Halton possesses the remains of an 11th-century castle, whilst at nearby Norton Priory – which was built by Augustinian friars in 1155 – there is a tasteful and informative museum, together with attractive gardens.

In the days before the developing town of Runcorn had merged with the village of Halton, the Barge was a farmhouse called Halton Gate Farm which occupied a rather isolated position on the banks of the Bridgewater Canal.

As the inn is owned by Bass the liquid refreshment draws on all the company's products, together with a varied offering of lagers and soft drinks. The ever-changing range of food is also most comprehensive. The 'Waterside Diner' is a restaurant where there are assorted starters, steaks and grills, various chicken and fish dishes and many desserts. Apart from the restaurant, more informal bar snacks can be purchased and choices are listed on a blackboard. These are good value and are constantly varied to suit the seasons. Speciality sandwiches are also on offer and are a meal in themselves. Again, these change throughout the year. Bar food is available every lunchtime from Monday to Friday between 12 noon and

2.30 pm and during the evening between 6 pm and 7 pm. The restaurant is also open throughout the week and in the evenings between 7 pm and 9.30 pm (9 pm on Sunday). Accompanied children are made welcome and can use the facilities up to 9.30 pm. Outside, there is a flagged area where tables and benches can be enjoyed when the weather is fine.
Telephone: 01928 566042.

How to get there: The A558 connects Runcorn with Higher Walton. This road can be accessed from either junction 11 or 12 off the M56 motorway. The Barge is situated at Halton Gate, just off the A558, 2 miles to the east of Runcorn.

Parking: There is a large car park at the Barge. Alternatively, there are parking facilities close to the entrance of Norton Priory Museum and Gardens.

Length of the walk: 2 miles. Map: OS Landranger 108 Liverpool (inn GR 543828).

Norton Priory Museum and Gardens are a delightful and intriguing place for a family visit. There are 16 acres of fascinating gardens to meander through – as well as interesting historical remains to observe and learn about. The approach to the site involves a stroll along the towpath of the Bridgewater Canal, the first major canal development in England, which played such an important role in the Industrial Revolution in Britain.

The Walk
From the inn join the towpath of the adjacent canal and turn right to pass under a road bridge.
You are now walking alongside the famous canal that ushered in the canal age and, with it, the Industrial Revolution in Britain. The Bridgewater Canal was engineered by James Brindley to distribute coal from the Duke of Bridgewater's estates at Worsley, near Manchester. The canal, which was completed in 1770, entered the Mersey through a series of locks at Runcorn.
Over to the right can be seen a lake, within Town Park, where visitors can relax and meander.
Keep along the towpath and arrive at a small brick bridge, Greens Bridge, which passes over the canal. Leave the canal here and walk over the bridge. Follow a cinder track which skirts the edge of a sports field.
Straight ahead, on the skyline, can be seen the huge cooling towers of Fiddler's Ferry Power Station. The track takes you to the car park

14

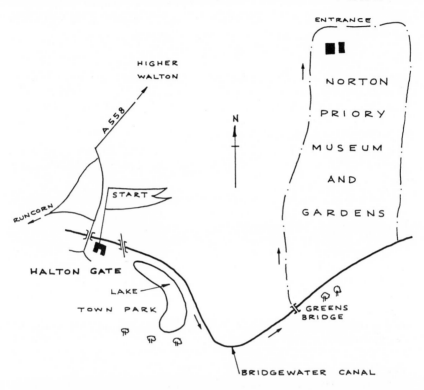

and ornate entrance gates of Norton Priory Museum. An inscription on the gates says: 'These gates were made and presented by the Widnes Foundry and Engineering Company in the 29th year of the reign of Queen Elizabeth II'.

The museum and gardens are contained within an area of 16 acres stretching back to the banks of the Bridgewater Canal. The museum, which is close by the site entrance, houses an exhibition of finds and there is a video to give an introduction to the site. Nearby, there are excavated remains and a medieval undercroft.

The beautiful landscaped woodland gardens, which once formed part of the grounds of the priory, are a joy through all the seasons. There is also a herb garden where plants common to the medieval period are cultivated. Numerous pathways through the trees give access to many varied features, one of which is the stream glade with its azaleas, rhododendrons, primulas and many wild plants. A summerhouse

15

Towpath on the Bridgewater Canal section.

contains an exhibition which relates the history of the gardens. Close by
there is a Victorian rock garden, near the banks of the Bridgewater Canal.
Many different species of birds are encouraged to visit the site and these
can be observed from a special hide. The interesting and unusual trees
are constantly being added to as the years go by. There is also a walled
garden to explore.

Norton Priory Museum and Gardens are open on weekdays from
12 noon to 5 pm, and at weekends and on bank holidays from 12 noon
to 6 pm – April to October inclusive. From November to March the
opening time is 12 noon to 4 pm every day. A modestly priced booklet
can be purchased which relates the history and development of the site.
Telephone for information: 01928 569895.

On leaving the site, retrace your way back to Greens Bridge and rejoin
the canal towpath for the stroll back to the Barge.

You may wish to spend some time, before returning to the car,
meandering around the adjacent lake and Town Park.

3 Knutsford
The Rose and Crown Hotel

The name Knutsford is said to be derived from the Danish king, Canute (or Knut). The town boasts a mix of architecture; mainly Georgian, but there are also Italian and Oriental influences to be seen. Close to the town is the great estate of Tatton, where 2,000 acres of lush parkland surround a mansion and contain a hall, working farm, formal gardens and two large meres. Without doubt one of the most interesting of Cheshire's towns, Knutsford possesses many hostelries to suit every taste.

The Rose and Crown is situated in the shadow of the Gaskell Memorial Tower, which was erected in 1907 in memory of the novelist Elizabeth Gaskell. The premises, primarily a wine bar and restaurant, have a distinctive continental feel and children are made welcome. A wide range of red and white wines can be purchased – by the bottle, or by the glass if preferred – and there is usually a good house wine on offer. A large number of English and European beers and lagers are also available.

The choice of food is just as comprehensive. There are 15 starters, including spare ribs, avocado with prawns, Parma ham and melon, stuffed peppers and Salade du Val – garlic croutons topped with mild French cheese, grilled and served on a bed of mixed leaves. There are

17

Deer in Tatton Park.

also many pasta dishes to select from, with spaghetti presented in a number of ways, as well as lasagne, tagliatelle and macaroni. Seven different types of pizza are available, too, and a choice of salads. Main courses, served with a selection of vegetables and potatoes, include roast breast of duck, rack of lamb, fillet, sirloin and rump steaks, veal, beef, scampi, and prawn dishes. To conclude a meal there is a daily-changing selection of tempting desserts and cheeses. On Sunday a very reasonably priced roast or fish meal is on offer.

Food is available every day from Monday to Saturday between 12 noon and 2.30 pm and in the evening between 6 pm and 10 pm. On Sunday food is served from 12 noon right through until 10 pm.

Telephone: 01565 652366.

How to get there: Knutsford lies on the main A50 road which connects Warrington with Holmes Chapel, and is five minutes' drive from junction 19 on the M6 motorway. The Rose and Crown is on King Street in the centre of town.

Parking: There is a car park at the rear of the inn – access to which is off Princess Street. Alternatively, there are numerous car parks in Knutsford and also within the Tatton Park Estate.

Length of the walk: 4¹/₂ miles. Map: OS Landranger 118 Stoke-on-Trent and Macclesfield (inn GR 752786).

There are two main ingredients to this walk – the historic town of Knutsford and Tatton Park Estate. Knutsford is a place where at least an hour should be given to strolling down its two main streets and exploring the narrow alleys which lead off them. The great park at Tatton is where the walker is given a glimpse of an environment which is hundreds of years old and time should be allowed for visiting the mansion, Old Hall, working farm and gardens.

From 1st April to 30th September, Tatton Park is open every day. From 1st October to 31st March the park is closed on Monday. The opening times for the various attractions vary with the seasons. Telephone: 01565 750250.

The Walk

Emerge from the Rose and Crown and turn left to walk along King Street. Pass the Royal George Hotel and continue past Minshull Street and the Angel Hotel. On passing Drury Lane – where the Italianate architecture of the Ruskin Rooms can be seen on the right – bear right to follow a gravel path between trees. The path takes you onto the entrance drive of Tatton Park, which you enter through the Town Entrance Arch.

Go through a gate on the left, which allows you to bypass a cattle-grid. Do not follow the macadam drive, but keep to the left to follow a well-defined path through trees. The path takes you between two rows of widely planted beech trees and is aptly named Beech Avenue. This was the course of the original entrance drive to the mansion. Over a fence on the left can be seen the neatly cut acres of Knutsford Golf Club. Continue along the path between the beech trees and emerge at a facing monument which is called The Temple. Keep to the right now and follow a well-defined track where there is a low concrete wall on the immediate right at first. There is a pleasant view here across to the smaller of the estate's two lakes, Melchett Mere.

Where the low wall finishes there is a junction of broad, grassy paths. Keep to the left here and follow a path which stays close to the trees on the left. There are glimpses of the mansion through the trees on the left now. The path turns to the left and joins a macadam drive which takes you to the front of it. This point is to be remembered as a navigational reference point for your return journey. The way straight ahead is clearly signed to various points of interest and attractions.

Having completed your visit to the various attractions, return to the front of the mansion. Follow the drive away from the house and, after 80 metres, arrive at a junction. The drive to the left goes to the Rostherne

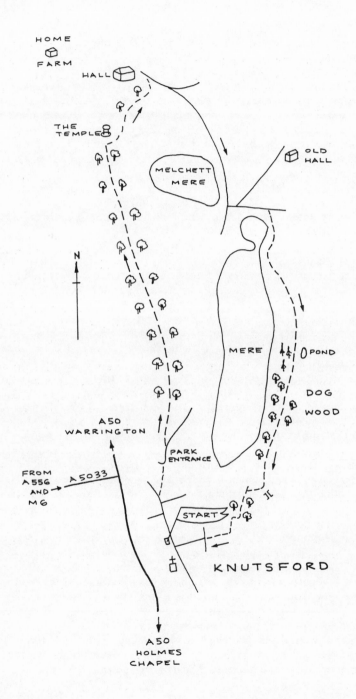

HOME FARM

HALL

THE TEMPLE

MELCHETT MERE

OLD HALL

N

MERE

POND

DOG WOOD

A50
WARRINGTON

PARK ENTRANCE

FROM A556 AND M6

A 5033

START

KNUTSFORD

A50
HOLMES CHAPEL

Exit, but keep right here in the direction of Old Hall. The drive takes you past Melchett Mere. On reaching the end of the lake, there is a junction of ways. The way straight ahead leads to the Knutsford Exit, but keep left here, again towards Old Hall. After only 30 metres there is a way on the left which goes to Old Hall (if time allows, a visit can be made to this 500 year old dwelling), but, to continue the walk, keep forward here in the direction of Tatton Outdoor Sailing Centre (T.O.S.C.).

On the right here and close by the water's edge, there is an information board which relates how, in 1982, a young boy from Knutsford discovered some flints in the area. This find led to the discovery of a Mesolithic, or Middle Stone Age, site – the earliest prehistoric settlement of its kind so far excavated in Britain.

A little further on, turn right where a notice says, 'Sailors' vehicles only'. Follow a gravel track passing close to the edge of the mere. In the far distance, and across the water, there is a long view to Knutsford – with one of its churches dominant. Cross a small car park and continue along a grassy path which generally follows the edge of the mere. Go through a gate in a crossing fence and keep along a broad, grassy path which gradually takes you further away from the water, to the right of a low sunken pond and past a small enclosed copse of conifer trees.

The path leads into Dog Wood, where you join a facing gravel track, which takes you through the trees. A storage area for sailing boats is over to the left here. Keep forward along the main track and pass through a large kissing-gate (this gate is locked every evening at 7 pm). Emerge from Dog Wood over a stile at the side of a facing gate. There is a junction of ways now. To the left a rough macadam path leads over a railway bridge, but keep forward here, to follow a narrow path which gradually descends through undergrowth.

At the bottom of the descent, turn left along a crossing path. Shortly, there is a junction of ways. Keep forward here, over a stile in a short section of fence between two adjacent trees, to follow the higher ground through trees where a banking slopes away to your right. Shortly, the path turns to the right, and then left, around a fenced-in compound. Where the fencing finishes, turn right to follow a path across a grassy common – where the bulk of Knutsford town can be seen dominating the elevated ground straight ahead. Over to the right there is a small lake called The Moor – whose waters are fed from Tatton Mere. Gently climb, across the town centre car park, and arrive back at King Street, close to the Rose and Crown.

4 Great Budworth
The George and Dragon

The village of Great Budworth, which overlooks Budworth Mere, sits on a hill three miles from the town of Northwich. Aptly, its name derives from Saxon times, meaning a dwelling by the water. The village is full of characterful cottages and seems to possess that idyllic charm of a way of life long since gone – hence the village is a popular location for films and television dramas.

At the heart of one of the most picturesque villages in Cheshire, the George and Dragon is situated opposite the village church and stocks. Constructed during 1722 as part of the Arley Estate, the inn is well known for its fine food, fine ales and fine hospitality.

Downstairs there are two bars, the Lounge Bar and Stocks Bar, where hot and cold food is served daily at lunchtimes and during the evening. Situated on the first floor is the Horseshoe Dining Room and family eating area, open mainly at weekends and during busier periods, where tables can be reserved in advance. A comprehensive menu is on offer, together with a 'Daily Specials' board. The appetisers include dim-sum, garlic mushrooms, prawn cocktail, pâté and the chef's soup of the day, followed by a wide selection of steaks, various curries, chicken, chilli and a traditional roast. Fish and seafood dishes are also available, as well as salads and vegetarian meals. You can order sandwiches, and there are children's and senior citizens' menus. The desserts include home-made apple pie, raspberry sponge, banana split and chocolate orange ice bombe. The meals can be complemented by a range of wines and liqueur coffees. The inn is a Tetley's house and hence serves their hand-pumped Bitter, together with two guest beers which are changed on a weekly basis. Addlestones draught cider can also be purchased, as well as a range of bottled beers and soft drinks. The inn has a no-smoking area, a family room and outside benches which can be utilised during warm weather.

Food is available at lunchtimes between 12 noon and 2.30 pm on Monday to Saturday, and on Sunday from 12 noon to 3 pm. During the evening food is served between 6.30 pm and 9.30 pm on Monday to Friday, and between 6 pm and 9.30 pm on Saturday and Sunday.

Telephone: 01606 891317.

How to get there: The A559 runs in a south-easterly direction from junction 10 of the M56 motorway and turns due west at Lostock Gralam to then pass through Northwich. Midway between the motorway and Lostock Gralam, and 1/4 mile to the east of the A559, is the village of Great Budworth – with the George and Dragon at its centre, opposite the church.

Parking: There is a car park at the rear of the inn. Alternatively, there is a car park, which is specifically for visitors, at Arley Hall.

Length of the walk: 5 miles. Map: OS Landranger 118 Stoke-on-Trent and Macclesfield (inn GR 664775).

This is the longest walk in the book and as there are no less than three attractions to visit at least five hours should be allowed for its completion. The main feature is Arley Hall and its 12 acres of magnificent award-winning gardens, and there is also an opportunity to sample some real Cheshire dairy ice cream and to visit a working farm. All this, coupled with a walk through beautiful countryside, combines to make for a memorable excursion.

The Walk

On leaving the inn, enter the facing School Lane, which commences at the side of the parish church of St Mary and All Saints. The tower of the church was erected in 1520 and is a fine example of early Cheshire architecture. The majority of the surrounding village houses were remodelled during the 19th century.

Follow a cobbled way between the church confines and a row of

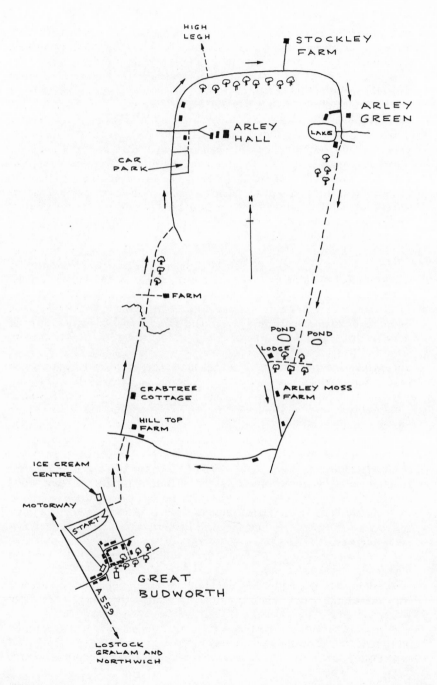

HIGH
LEGH

STOCKLEY
FARM

ARLEY
GREEN

ARLEY
HALL

LAKE

CAR
PARK

N

FARM

POND   POND

LODGE

CRABTREE
COTTAGE

ARLEY MOSS
FARM

HILL TOP
FARM

ICE CREAM
CENTRE

MOTORWAY

START

GREAT
BUDWORTH

A559

LOSTOCK
GRALAM AND
NORTHWICH

24

interesting black and white cottages. Pass Great Budworth school and enter a tree-lined path through a kissing-gate. There is a small sports field on the left here. Where the sports field finishes, turn left and walk away from the tree-lined path along a broad track. After 150 metres arrive at a crossing lane. Walk straight across the lane and enter a facing lane in the direction of Antrobus and Warrington. After 150 metres there is a stile on the right which gives access to a field. However, before crossing this stile continue along the lane for a further 60 metres to arrive at New Westage Farm, the Great Budworth Real Dairy Ice Cream Centre.

Freshly made ice cream is available in cartons and cones in various flavours, and there is a picnic area where customers can sit and enjoy their purchases. The centre is open from 1st April to 31st October daily from 12 noon to 6 pm, and during November and December at weekends from 1 pm to 5 pm (closed January to March). Telephone for information: 01606 891211.

Having sampled the ice cream, return along the lane to the stile, cross it, and enter a field. Follow the edge of the field, keeping a fence on your immediate right. At the field corner turn left and continue, now with a hedge on your immediate right. Go over a facing stile to enter a large field. Walk along the field edge, keeping a fence on your left. On reaching the field corner, go over a stile, cross a lane and enter a concrete drive which is headed by a sign which says: 'Private no entry, Footpath Only'. The drive takes you past a dwelling called Crabtree Cottage. Pass through a gate and follow a straight stretch of drive for 400 metres to arrive at a gate. Go over a stile at the side of the gate and continue along a field edge, keeping a hedge on your immediate right. A stile at the field corner gives access to a small wood where a well-defined path leads through the trees and to a footbridge which takes you over Arley Brook. On crossing the footbridge turn left and quickly emerge from the trees through a small gate which takes you into a large field. Follow the field edge, keeping a fence and hedge on your immediate right. Pass over a stile at the field corner and go straight over a crossing track which leads to a farm on the right.

A facing stile gives access to another field, where the footpath follows its right-hand edge close to a hedge and fence. Go over another stile and continue, with a wood on your right side. Where the trees finish there is another stile to negotiate, after which the route is along a field edge, keeping a fence on your immediate right. The path takes you to a crossing lane via a stile at the side of a gate. Turn left and follow a straight length of lane, which runs between fences through the Arley Estate. Arrive at the car park of Arley Hall, which is on the right.

The pedestrian entrance to Arley Hall and Gardens commences in the corner of the car park, where a gravel track takes you to a crossing lane. Turn right here, then fork right, to follow a tree-lined approach towards

Arley Hall.

a facing building, on top of which there is a large clock, and arrive at the entrance kiosk to Arley Hall and Gardens.

Arley is justifiably well known for its beautiful gardens and particularly for the herbaceous borders, which were among the first to be established in England. Apart from the borders, another remarkable feature is an avenue of 14 holm oaks which were planted in 1840 and have been clipped to resemble giant cylinders. In more recent years, the Hall itself has been open to the public and is a fine example of the early-Victorian, Jacobean style, built on the site of an earlier building dating back to 1190. Apart from the Hall and gardens there is a chapel and a gift shop, and a restaurant sited in a former Tudor barn which once served as stables. The gardens are open from April until the end of September, Tuesday to Sunday inclusive, as well as bank holidays, between 12 noon and 5 pm. The opening times for the Hall vary. Telephone for information: 01565 777353.

On leaving the Hall and gardens walk past the gravel track which leads to the car park and arrive at a crossroads. Turn right here, where a rather intriguing old wooden sign says: 'No cartway save on sufferance here, for horse and foot the road is clear, to Lymm, High Legh, Hoo Green and Mere'. Another, more mundane, sign says: 'Bridleroad Only'.

Follow the lane as it gradually bends to the right and keep on past a track on the left which goes to High Legh. A little further on, on the left, is the entrance drive of Stockley Farm – our third, and final, attraction of the day.

Here children are encouraged to stroke, cuddle and help to feed the animals. The cows can be watched while being milked and there is a gift shop to browse in and a picnic and play area. The farm is open from April until early October every Wednesday, Saturday, Sunday and on bank holidays, and every day during August, except Monday. Telephone for information: 01565 777323.

On leaving the farm, walk back up the entrance drive and turn left to continue along the lane. The way becomes cobbled for a short distance and takes you into the attractive hamlet of Arley Green – with its water pump, cottages and the half-timbered building of the old school house at the far side of the green. Go over Arley Brook, with a lake on the right. The lane turns sharply to the left now, but keep forward along a short stretch of track at the side of a dwelling to cross a stile at the right-hand side of a facing field gate. Follow the edge of a large field, keeping trees on your immediate right. At the corner go over a stile and continue along the edge of the next field. The footpath, which is waymarked by yellow arrows, continues in the same general direction and takes you across five fields and over a mixture of stiles and plank bridges to where you enter trees via a stile.

Follow a well-defined path through the trees and after 30 metres turn right at a crossing path. After 80 metres of tree-lined path arrive at a lane via a stile at the side of a facing gate. On the right there is a lodge-gate entrance to Arley Estate, but turn left along the lane and walk away from the lodge.

Pass Arley Moss Farm and continue to a junction, where the way is to the right, in the direction of Great Budworth and Northwich. After 120 metres turn right to enter Budworth Heath Lane. Pass Crossfield House and after ½ mile arrive at Hill Top Farm, on the right. Almost opposite the farm entrance there is a footpath, which begins over a stile set in a hedge on the left. Cross the stile and continue along the edge of a large field, keeping a fence on your immediate right.

You are now back on part of your initial route. Follow the footpath to the lane close to the ice cream centre and then turn left to arrive at a junction of lanes. As an alternative, you may wish to turn right here and follow the laneside pavement back into Great Budworth to arrive back at the George and Dragon and the car.

5 Anderton
The Stanley Arms

At the heart of the age old Cheshire salt industry, Anderton developed hand in hand with the Industrial Revolution. The construction of the Trent and Mersey Canal, and its link with the nearby river Weaver via the gigantic lift, known as the Anderton Lift, was one of the engineering feats of its time. Apart from its associations with industrial development, Anderton is close to a lovely tract of countryside at Marbury Park – which overlooks Budworth Mere to the south of Great Budworth village.

Dating back to the early 18th century – at which time it was the home of the Stanley family – these premises provided succour for those involved with the construction of the adjacent canal. The association with the canal accounts for the inn being known locally as 'the Tip', as salt from the nearby salt works used to be tipped into canal barges in the vicinity. The internal decor confirms this connection, for the walls are adorned with paintings and photographs depicting canal scenes.

The inn belongs to Greenalls and dispenses two types of cask real ale, their own and a version brewed by Stones. Mild and bitter beers are available, together with draught Scrumpy Jack and Strongbow ciders. Meals, which are prepared to order, include home-made steak and kidney pie, deep-fried chicken, gammon – with egg or with pineapple – breaded scampi, quiche, jumbo sausage, lasagne, battered cod and various salads. For those who prefer something more spicy, there is Mexican chilli con carne or chicken curry. Soup is also served, together with a range of sandwiches, hot toasties and various omelettes. The sweet trolley presents a wide variety and there is also a comprehensive menu devoted to children. The inn has a large beer garden, together with an adjoining play area. There is a family room and a conservatory-style extension to the dining area which overlooks the beer garden and play area.

The inn is open every day for meals between 12 noon and 2 pm and in the evening between 6.30 pm and 9 pm, except on Sunday, when the evening starting time is 7 pm.

Telephone: 01606 75059.

How to get there: The village of Anderton lies 1 mile to the north-west of Northwich, just off the A533 Northwich to Runcorn road. The Stanley Arms is situated on Old Road, close to the Trent and Mersey Canal.

Parking: There is a car park in front of the inn. Alternatively, there are numerous parking places in Marbury Country Park.

Length of the walk: 3 miles. Map: OS Landranger 118 Stoke-on-Trent and Macclesfield (inn GR 647753).

There are constant reminders of our national heritage on this walk. Marbury Country Park with its expanses of lush green meadows, waterside gardens and belts of trees can boast a history going back almost 1,000 years. In contrast, the massive civil engineering works made possible by the Industrial Revolution, and later developed during the Victorian era, are equally impressive. This circuit presents an opportunity to combine a visit to the ancient park at Marbury with a stroll along a section of the Trent and Mersey Canal, prior to concluding the walk with a look at one of the engineering feats of the last century – the Anderton Lift.

The Walk

Leave the inn and turn left to climb gradually up Old Road. Arrive at the main road close by Walkers of Cheshire (a local travel company). Turn left, but after only 40 metres cross the road to enter a track where there is a footpath sign. After 50 metres bear right and cross a stile at the right hand side of a field gate. Follow a path which crosses a field, bearing right, in the direction of a stile which can be seen straight ahead. Follow a straight stretch of footpath and cross three stiles. On crossing the third

29

stile, aim for a small detached dwelling which can be seen across the field, again straight ahead. A stile gives access to a lane, where the way is left. After 150 metres, and 30 metres before the entrance drive of Claycroft Farm, go over a stile on the right, where there is a footpath sign.

Gradually descend across two fields and cross over two stiles. Enter trees and traverse Marbury Brook via a stout footbridge. Emerge from the trees over a stile and then follow a field edge. After 100 metres, go over a stile to join a road. Cross the road and turn right to follow the roadside pavement. After only 50 metres turn left to enter a wide, rough, macadam drive, which takes you into trees. Keep to the left of a facing crossing gate and then follow the drive when it bends to the right.

You have now entered Marbury Country Park – a parkland area covering over 200 acres. Within the park there are picnic sites and information boards which relate to various points of interest. This glorious parkland setting once formed the estate of Marbury Hall, alas now demolished, and we are very fortunate to be allowed access to such a beautiful expanse of countryside. Steps on the left lead down to the edge of Budworth Mere, where a slotted partition has been erected allowing visitors to observe the wildlife. An information board nearby describes all the various species of birds and plantlife to be seen hereabouts. Follow a path which takes you through trees and generally stays parallel with the shoreline of the mere. Keep to the left where the path forks. Descend steps and pass close to a boathouse to follow a path along the very edge of the water.

Across the mere, over to the right, can be seen the tower of Great Budworth church – quite a splendid sight throughout all the seasons of the year. Arrive at a miniature beach, close to where there are facing stone steps. Do not ascend these steps, but turn right, and climb along a rough, wide track which leads away from the waterside. On reaching more level terrain, the way is forward along a narrow bridleway, where there is a fence on the right and trees on the left. The path bends to the left and cuts through the trees for a short distance to continue, again with a fence on the right and trees on the left. Follow the path as it kinks around the edge of the trees. On meeting a T-junction of paths, turn right to follow a wide, fenced-in path. Continue until a crossing lane is reached, where the way is left. You have now emerged from Marbury Country Park.

Follow the lane for 400 metres to arrive at a bridge which takes you over the canal. Leave the lane here to the left and descend steps to arrive on the towpath. Turn left and pass under the bridge you have just walked over.

The canal was planned by James Brindley and was constructed during the 18th century, initially to carry china clay between Liverpool and the Potteries, and later for the distribution of Cheshire salt. (A visit to the

30

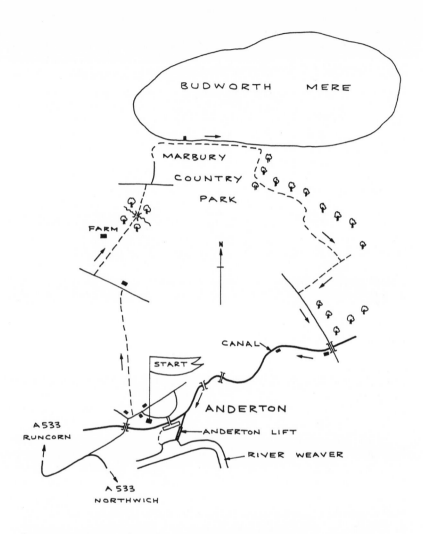

Salt Museum in Northwich and the Lion Salt Works at nearby Marston, will reveal why Cheshire is at the heart of the British salt industry.)

Pass a delightful waterside dwelling called Jackson's Turn, and on reaching the Anderton Marina, continue along a section of lane which stays parallel with the canal. Do not cross bridge 198, but descend steps to its left to continue along the canal towpath once again. Pass under bridge 199. The next bridge across the canal is a footbridge and this leads back to Old Road, where the way is left, back to the Stanley Arms. However, it would be a pity to conclude the walk without first having

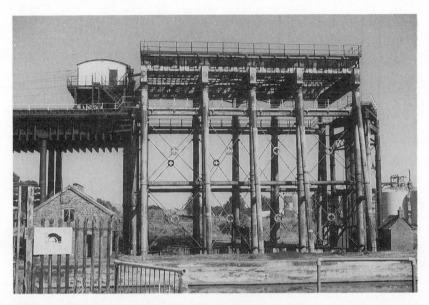

The Anderton Lift, completed in 1875.

sight of one of the engineering masterpieces of canal design. Instead of crossing to the other side of the canal, descend from the footbridge and take a path which descends through trees on the left. At the bottom of the descent there is an excellent view of the massive structure of the Anderton Lift.

The lift, which was completed during 1875, was constructed to transfer barges between the canal and the river Weaver. The lift contains two tanks, each capable of carrying 252 tons of water, to transport the barges between the two waterways over a height difference of 50 ft. Originally, this was carried out using a system of hydraulic rams; however, the lift was electrified during 1908. Although it is currently out of use, work is being undertaken with a view to restoring it to its former glory.

Having viewed this engineering feat of the Victorian age, return to the canal, cross the footbridge, and turn left to walk back to the Stanley Arms.

Whiteley Green
The Windmill Inn

Situated at the point where the foothills of the Peak District meet the Cheshire Plain, the area around Whiteley Green is truly idyllic. Nearby Bollington is also blessed with the good fortune to have lovely views from almost every dwelling and an interesting Discovery Centre which is set in the gate lodge of a now defunct textile mill.

The attractive Windmill Inn enjoys an enviable location and is set within 3 acres of garden close to the Macclesfield Canal. The building was once a farmhouse, the origins of which date back to the 16th century. Its interior is heavily beamed and there are many quiet corners in which to relax. The facilities include a no-smoking area, a beer garden, a family room and a play area for children. During the summer various attractions are arranged in the garden area and there is an outside bar and barbecue.

The inn has built up an excellent reputation for its food and a most comprehensive menu is on offer, together with a specials board. The starters include prawn cocktail, speciality soup, garlic mushrooms, chicken satay, cheesy garlic bread and a wide choice of 7 inch traditional Yorkshire puddings. There are poultry and fish dishes and a choice of vegetarian meals, as well as various types and sizes of steaks and an extensive cold table. Mixed grill, gammon steak and a variety of sandwiches are also on offer. All the main courses are served with chipped or jacket potatoes and mixed vegetables. A range of tempting desserts includes hot chocolate fudge cake, banana split, apple pie, sherry trifle, and lots of different ice creams. Real ales, among them Tetley, Pedigree and Imperial, can be purchased and there is always a guest beer available, together with various ciders and a large selection of soft drinks.

Meals are served on Monday to Saturday from 12 noon to 2.30 pm and 7 pm to 11 pm. On Sunday food is available from 12 noon throughout the afternoon and evening.

Telephone: 01625 574222.

How to get there: The A523 connects Macclesfield with Poynton. Midway between these two places, that is about 3½ miles to the north of Macclesfield and close to where the railway runs parallel to the road, there is a sign which points along Holehouse Lane and tells you that Whiteley Green is 1 mile away. Drive down the lane to arrive at the Windmill Inn, which is on the right.

Parking: There is a car park at the rear of the inn. There is also a car park, which is specifically for visitors, at Bollington Discovery Centre.

Length of the walk: 3 miles. Map: OS Landranger 118 Stoke-on-Trent and Macclesfield (inn GR 925789).

Apart from providing an opportunity to meander through pleasant scenery, the walk has strong links with the history of transport. The first half of the walk is along a section of the Middlewood Way, which follows the course of an old railway line and takes you to the Bollington Discovery Centre. The return leg is along the towpath of an interesting stretch of the Macclesfield Canal which provides a fine platform for magnificent views across to the foothills of the Peak District.

The Walk
On leaving the inn, turn right and gradually climb along Holehouse Lane. After 200 metres, arrive at a bridge. Leave the lane to the right here to descend steps which take you onto a level path. Turn right and walk away from the bridge.

You have joined the Middlewood Way, which was opened in 1985 and follows the course of an old railway line that once connected Macclesfield with Marple.

Keep forward along the main path, ignoring other routes which go off to the left and right. Pass under a bridge and continue. The route takes

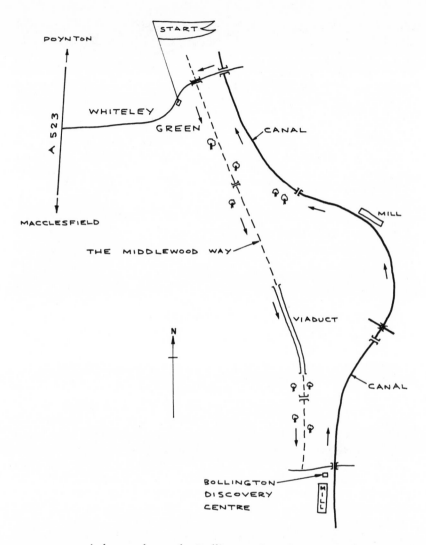

you across a viaduct and past the Bollington Arts Centre. Having crossed the viaduct, pass under a bridge and continue along the main path, which gradually descends and leads to Grimshaw Lane. Turn left now, pass Clough Bank, and arrive at Bollington Discovery Centre, which is on the right, set in the former gate lodge of the adjacent Adelphi Mill, which closed for textile production in 1975, and now houses a range of small businesses and a hotel. The Centre hosts a series of changing exhibitions on themes such as local history, local crafts, wildlife and the

35

The Bollington Discovery Centre.

environment, with related talks and events. There is also a small gift shop. Cycles can be rented and canoe hire is available on the adjacent canal. The opening times are 2 pm to 4.30 pm on Monday to Friday and 11 am to 4.30 pm at weekends. Admission is free. Telephone for information: 01625 572681.

On leaving the Discovery Centre, ascend a flight of steps to arrive on the towpath of the canal. Turn left and pass an information board which tells you all about Adelphi Mill. Walk under bridge 27 and follow the canal as it traverses a road which can be spotted down on the left. You are now approaching Clarence Mill, whose tall, red-bricked chimney can be seen straight ahead. Follow the canal as it turns to the left and pass the large façade of Clarence Mill.

Built in the 1820s, contemporary with the canal, the mill was closed during the 1960s and now houses small industrial units. A nearby information board relates its history.

Pass under bridge 26 and continue to the next bridge, 25. Leave the canal towpath just before the bridge, to the left, and ascend a flight of steps to reach a lane. Turn left. Pass over the Middlewood Way via a bridge, and after a further 200 metres arrive back at the Windmill Inn and the car.

7 Ness
The Wheatsheaf

The attractive village of Ness sits atop a hill overlooking the Dee estuary. Close by are the famous Ness Gardens, which take advantage of a reasonably temperate climate to produce a show of colour throughout all the seasons of the year.

The Wheatsheaf is a large pub which is situated in the centre of the village. Inside, there are a number of tiered rooms and ornamental stained-glass windows depicting the wheatsheaf emblem.

Thwaites real ales are available from the bar. Food is available every lunchtime from 12 noon to 2.30 pm during the week and 12 noon to 2 pm on Saturday and Sunday. There is a choice of starters, hot snacks, sandwiches and salads. The main courses include grilled gammon and pineapple or egg, roast chicken, golden scampi, breaded plaice and steak and kidney pie – all served with chipped or jacket potatoes and a choice of vegetables and garnish. Among the sweets are hot chocolate fudge cake, apple pie and treacle sponge. Children are welcome and smaller portions are offered. There is a large, lawned picnic area with tables – which can be utilised when the weather is fine – and a children's play area.

Telephone: 0151 336 2150.

How to get there: The A540 connects Chester with Hoylake on the Wirral peninsula. Approximately midway there is a secondary road which runs in a westerly direction from the A540 and is headed by a sign for 'Ness Gardens'. Continue past the entrance to the gardens to arrive at the village of Ness, and the Wheatsheaf.

Parking: There is a large car park at the side of the Wheatsheaf. There is also an extensive parking area, which is specifically for visitors, at Ness Gardens.

Length of the walk: 3 miles. Map: OS Landranger 117 Chester (inn GR 302760).

This walk provides an opportunity to 'take the sea air' and have a close look at the interesting, ornamental Ness Gardens – resplendent throughout all the seasons of the year. The walk takes you from the village of Ness to the gardens, and then along the shoreline of the Dee estuary, where wildfowl are to be seen in abundance.

The Walk

On leaving the inn, follow the roadside pavement in the direction of Ness Gardens, signposted. Pass Mill Lane and continue past Smith's Cottages, which are raised above the road level and are built on a solid base of sandstone rock. Where the pavement finishes, keep on along the roadside verge for a short distance before rejoining the pavement. Shortly after passing Haddon Lane, which goes off to the left, arrive at the entrance to Ness Gardens. The gardens are open daily from March to October between 9.30 am and dusk and from November to February between 9.30 am and 4 pm. Telephone for information: 0151 353 0123.

On leaving the gardens, turn right, and continue along the roadside pavement. Turn next right and descend along Denhall Lane. This is a good platform for long views straight ahead across the Dee estuary to the hills of North Wales. The lane takes you over the railway and past the entrance to Denna Hall. Turn right now, to follow another lane, where a footpath sign points towards 'Quayside'.

On your immediate left are the silted up edges of the Dee estuary and it is difficult to imagine that the waters of the river Dee actually flowed along here in days gone by.

The lane becomes a track for a short distance and then takes you past a farm. The macadam surface finishes by the entrance to a transmitting station – but keep forward here, along the facing grassy track, which finishes at a gate. Pass through the gate and follow a path which hugs a fence on the right. On the left here is a wet, marshy area which is a favourite haunt of bird-watchers.

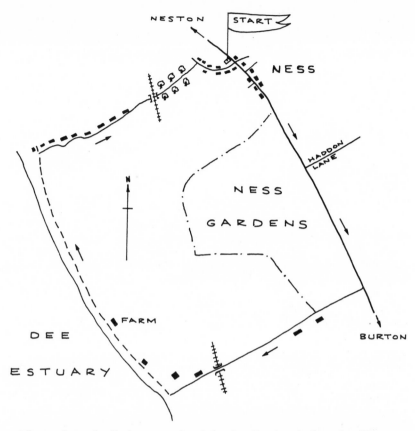

The path gradually bears to the right shortly, just before dwellings are reached. Turn right now to follow a macadam path, which begins where a short concrete post is set into the ground. The path takes you around the edge of fairly new property. Keep to the right at a junction of paths and continue past the dwellings, which are on your left. Where the paths diverge, keep forward to pass between metal barriers, which are set about one metre apart. The path takes you past the rear of some bungalows. Turn right at a facing fence and immediately go over a stile, to continue in the same direction as before. Go over another stile and then walk forward to follow a track, which takes you under the railway.

The track gradually climbs between trees and hedges. At the top, and opposite dwellings called New Heys and Willow Croft, turn right to follow a lane. On passing Well Close arrive back at the Wheatsheaf and the car.

8 Mouldsworth
The Goshawk

The undulating tract of countryside between Frodsham and Kelsall presents an opportunity for long vistas towards the Peckforton Hills, and beyond. At its heart is the sprawling village of Mouldsworth, where there is the added attraction of a motor museum which is a mecca for those with an interest in transport.

Situated at the edge of Delamere Forest, the Goshawk was once called the Station Hotel – due to its location opposite the village railway station. It is ideal for families, having a large family room with play facilities and a huge adventure playground at the rear. There is a finely manicured bowling green surrounded by seats and tables and internally there are a number of comfortable rooms.

Ale from the cask includes Greenalls and Theakston and there is a guest beer which is changed weekly. The usual array of mild, bitter and ciders is also available and there is a wide choice of soft drinks for children to choose from. Meals are served every day at lunchtime and during the evening. Starters include soup, pâté, deep-fried mushrooms and prawn cocktail. Among the main dishes are steak and ale pie, gammon steak, chicken Kiev, roast chicken, various steaks and the Big Grill – a mixture of steak, gammon, lamb chop, sausage, fried egg, grilled tomato and onion rings. Then there are hot 'n' spicy offerings, such as chicken tikka masala, hot chilli pot and lasagne Romano. A variety of fish dishes and salad platters can also be purchased. There is also a board proclaiming daily specials. A very keenly priced roast Sunday lunch is served every week from 12 noon. A wide choice of desserts is offered, as well as tea and various coffees – including Goshawk Special Coffee, freshly brewed, topped with whipped cream and served with a chocolate flake.

Telephone: 01928 740302.

How to get there: The B5393 runs for about 7 miles between the A56 at Frodsham and the A54 near Kelsall and passes through the sprawling village of Mouldsworth, which sits atop a hill, 2 miles from the A54. The Goshawk is close to the top of the hill, opposite the railway station.

Parking: There are car parks at the front and rear of the inn. Alternatively, there are parking facilities at Mouldsworth Motor Museum.

Length of the walk: 3 miles. Map: OS Landranger 117 Chester (inn GR 511707).

Deep in the heart of the Cheshire countryside, close by the wooded expanse of Delamere Forest, seems an unlikely location for a motor museum. However, this very situation means that an interesting visit can be coupled with a circular walk through some choice Cheshire scenery, which can be viewed from a combination of field paths, tracks and leafy lanes.

The Walk

From the inn cross the road, turn left and follow the roadside pavement to climb gradually. On reaching more level ground, turn left opposite a dwelling called The Rookery and cross the road to go over a stile at the side of a field gate. Follow a field edge, keeping a fence on your immediate right. Go over another stile and follow a facing track which takes you to a crossing lane. Turn right and, after only 30 metres, turn left to enter a hedged-in track which commences almost opposite the village police station. A straight 80 metres takes you to a facing gate where there are stables beyond. Do not go through this facing gate, but turn right to pass through another gate and follow a short section of fenced-in path. Go over a stile to enter a field. Cross the field then pass over a rather unusual stone stile. Turn left and then right to follow a field edge and walk to a stile which is at the left-hand side of a walled-in brick building that can be seen straight ahead (Mouldsworth Methodist

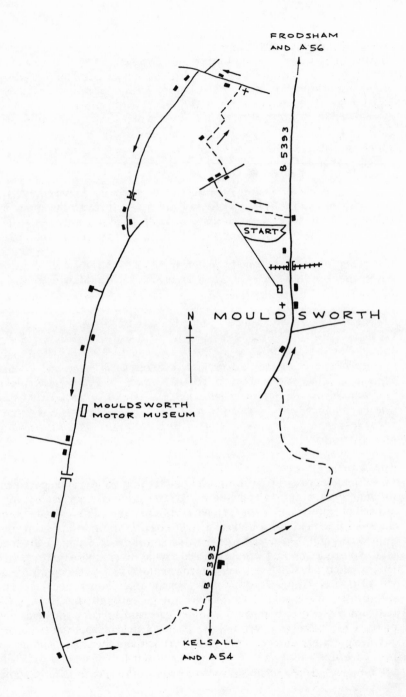

FRODSHAM
AND A56

B 5393

START

N

MOULDSWORTH

MOULDSWORTH
MOTOR MUSEUM

B 5393

KELSALL
AND A54

church). Cross the stile and enter Chapel Lane.

Turn left and continue along the laneside pavement. Pass Moss Lane – which goes off on the right towards Alvanley – and then immediately turn left to enter Well Lane. Gradually descend along this pleasant lane, which presents an excellent platform for long views towards the distant Peckforton Hills, and after $\frac{1}{2}$ mile arrive at a T-junction. Turn right and walk along the grass verge. Pass Mouldsworth Hall Farm and Poplar Grove to arrive shortly at the entrance to Mouldsworth Motor Museum, which is on the left.

The museum, which was established during 1971, is housed in a most unusual building. Constructed during 1937, it was initially used as a water-softening treatment centre. During the Second World War, the machinery was left idle due to a lack of manpower and many problems were encountered when attempting to bring it back into full working order. The difficulties were eventually resolved by bringing in soft water from the Birmingham area and mixing it with the main water supply – a process which is still carried on in the adjacent building. Hence, the museum was established following the removal of all the redundant water-softening machinery.

This is a mecca for anyone with an interest in the history of transport. There are examples of early motor cars and motor cycles, bicycles, pedal cars, Dinky toys, old tools, magazines and signs from a bygone age. The author's favourite exhibits are an E-type Jaguar, an Italian red Ferrari Dino and a fine example of an Austin A50, which reminds him of family days out during the 1950s. There is also a reconstruction of a 1920s garage – which really captures the ambience of an era long since gone.

The museum is open on Sunday and all bank holidays between 12 noon and 5 pm, from March to the end of November. It is also open on Wednesday from 1 pm to 5 pm throughout July and August. Telephone number: 01928 731781.

On leaving the museum, turn left and continue along the facing lane, ignoring a turn off to the right which goes to Dunham. Descend, go under a bridge, and continue past Brook House. On passing West View, go over a stile on the left where a footpath sign points away from the lane. This footpath commences opposite the entrance drive of Peel Hall. The path is fenced in at first, but on passing over a stile keep to the edge of a rough, undulating field, where there is a hedgerow on the immediate left. The spire of Ashton church can be seen peeping over the top of a banking on the right. Go over another stile then, a little further on, pass through a tall kissing-gate. The path follows the edge of a field, where there is now a hedgerow on your immediate right. Follow the path as it bends to the right, then go over a stile which takes you onto a road.

Turn left and, on passing Bottom Lodge, turn right to enter Grange

Motoring memorabilia at the Mouldsworth museum!

Road. Climb along this pleasant lane (it is far too narrow to be called a road). On passing the entrance drives to Grange House, Ashton Grange and Ashton Grange Cottage, the lane descends. After a further 50 metres, leave it by going over a stile on the left, where there is a footpath sign. Follow the edge of an undulating field, keeping a fence on your immediate right. On passing an electricity pole, the path enters undergrowth, then winds, and leads to a crossing road via a stile. Turn right and walk along the roadside verge. Pass Delamere Road – which goes off to the right – and climb along the roadside pavement. A few more strides and you are back at the Goshawk and the car.

9 Walker Barn
The Setter Dog

At the very edge of the Peak National Park, the countryside around Walker Barn can only be described as superb. The area also has long associations with quarrying, the history of which is related at the nearby Tegg's Nose Country Park.

Situated in a fold in the hills above Macclesfield and close to Macclesfield Forest, the Setter Dog at Walker Barn looks out over some magnificent scenery. Constructed during 1740, it was once the only establishment in England that performed the dual functions of both inn and post office. Apart from providing sustenance for travellers, it also served the needs of the workers at the nearby Tegg's Nose Quarry over many long years. The premises have a curious association with the nursery rhyme *Hey Diddle Diddle*, for it is said that the laughing dog mentioned referred to a pet once kept there.

The inn, which is built at an angle to suit the bend in the adjacent road, has a wood-panelled lounge fitted with bench seats and a separate dining room with wooden beams. Accompanied children are allowed inside and there is a beer garden which can be enjoyed when the weather is fine. Apart from Marston's Pedigree and Best Bitter, there is a cask guest ale which changes at least once a week. Draught Strongbow cider is also served, together with a wide range of bottled ales and soft drinks. The range of food is very comprehensive. There are dishes to suit every taste, varying from a choice of starters and vegetarian meals through grills, fish, pasta and curries to a delicious selection of desserts. A good and varied wine list is on offer.

On Monday to Saturday food is served every lunchtime between 11.30 am and 3 pm and during the evening between 5.30 pm and 10 pm. On Sunday food is available between 12 noon and 10.30 pm.

Telephone: 01625 431444.

How to get there: The A537 climbs out of Macclesfield and winds its way towards Buxton. About 3 miles from Macclesfield is the tiny hamlet of Walker Barn, with the Setter Dog in its midst.

Parking: There is a car park on the opposite side of the road from the inn. Alternatively, there is a large car park at Tegg's Nose Country Park, which is about ½ mile down the lane that commences opposite the inn.

Length of the walk: 2 miles. Map: OS Landranger 118 Stoke-on-Trent and Macclesfield (inn GR 956737).

This may be a very short walk, but the views unfolding during it are superb – across the Cheshire Plain to the Wrekin and the Welsh mountains to the west, Macclesfield Forest and the Derbyshire hills to the east, Croker Hill and Mow Cop to the south and the Pennines to the north. All this, coupled with the industrial history associated with Tegg's Nose Country Park, makes for a most enjoyable and rewarding excursion.

The Walk
Cross the road and enter a lane which commences directly opposite the inn, where a sign points towards 'Tegg's Nose'. (Take care here as the road is usually quite busy.) Keep on, past the tiny Walker Barn Methodist church, which was built in 1863 in a plain, simple, but strong, style. Gradually climb along the lane and, on reaching the crest of the hill, admire the wonderful views. Across to the left, above the wooded slopes, can be seen the summit of Shutlingsloe, whilst straight ahead there are long views across the Cheshire Plain. If the day is clear you should be able to see the huge dish of the radio telescope at Jodrell Bank in the middle distance over to the right.

Descend, and shortly arrive at the entrance to Tegg's Nose Country Park, where there is an Information Centre and parking facilities.

Before continuing with the described walk you may wish to obtain an information leaflet and perhaps ascend to the summit of Tegg's Nose

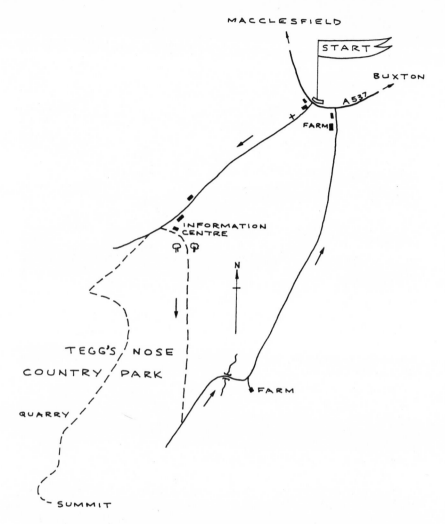

– the path to which begins to the right of the entrance gate. (The information leaflet also gives alternative walks which you may wish to complete or use to extend or vary the described route.)

Tegg's Nose Country Park has been developed around former quarries where the millstone grit was valued as a tough, but workable, building stone. Quarrying commenced during the Middle Ages and continued until 1955. During the 19th and early 20th centuries the area provided the setts and paving for the northern mill towns, whilst some of the high-quality stone was used to repair a number of the Cambridge University

A picnic site with views of the National Park.

colleges. At the foot of the quarry face there is a display showing how the stone was obtained and used. The name 'Tegg's Nose' apparently came into being because the original shape of the hill resembled the head of a young sheep which used to be called a 'Tegg'. For information about Tegg's Nose Country Park telephone: 01625 614279.

On passing the Information Centre, walk forward for a further 50 metres to arrive at the head of a path which commences close by a stone sign pointing to Langley and Forest Chapel. There is a display board close by which identifies various points of interest in the surrounding landscape.

Descend along the path, initially through trees, and along a rocky and then cobbled path where there are fine views towards Croker Hill, which is topped by a telecommunications mast. The path follows the route of an old packhorse trail known as Saddlers Way.

At the bottom of the descent turn sharply to the left and walk along a narrow lane. This takes you over Walker Barn stream and climbs past a farm entrance drive which goes off to the right. Again, there are magnificent views looking back across the surrounding countryside.

On reaching more level terrain there is a small farm on the left. Shortly after passing this farm, arrive at a crossing road. Turn left to arrive back at the Setter Dog and the car.

10 Peover Heath
The Dog Inn

The adjacent parishes of Over and Lower Peover can boast a long history. The name 'Peover' (pronounced peever) derives from the Anglo-Saxon 'Peeffer' – bright river, which refers to a stream called Peover Eye which meanders through the district. Unlike Lower Peover, Over Peover has no distinct centre and is scattered over a wide area.

The Dog Inn is situated in the parish of Over Peover, at the centre of the pleasant hamlet of Peover Heath. The inn has been known by several different names over the past 100 years. At the turn of the century the premises were called the New Inn, which was later changed to the Dog and Rot, rot being the local name for rat.

Internally, the inn is very attractive, with a number of different rooms and alcoves. Old photographs show scenes from the last century, one of which depicts a tinker's cart visiting the hostelry. There is a smoke-free dining area where children are most welcome, and a beer garden.

The owners remind the Dog's customers that it is not a restaurant, but a 'pub serving food', therefore the service is casual and friendly, which is reflected in the prices. Because of its reputation for providing such excellent value, it is advisable to book, as many people in the know travel long distances to sample the offerings. There is no set menu due to the fact that the choices are varied daily and to suit each changing season. The liquid refreshment is just as good as the food, with real ale from Jennings, Greenalls, Flowers and Tetley. There are different lagers and a range of ciders, including Addlestones cask conditioned cider. Also, there are over 60 different types of malt whisky from which to choose.

Lunch is served every day between 12 noon and 2.30 pm, and dinner between 7 pm and 9.30 pm. Overnight accommodation is also available. Telephone: 01625 861421.

How to get there: The hamlet of Peover Heath, with the Dog Inn at its centre, lies 4 miles to the south-east of Knutsford and is about 1½ miles from the A50, A535 and A537 roads. From the A50, follow a lane past the Whipping Stocks Inn and keep straight on past Ye Olde Park Gate Inn, to arrive at Peover Heath.

Parking: There is a large car park at the rear of the inn. Alternatively, there are parking facilities at Jodrell Bank Science Centre and Arboretum.

Length of the walk: 4 miles. Map: OS Landranger 118 Stoke-on-Trent and Macclesfield (inn GR 793736).

This is certainly a walk of contrasts – from an old inn deep in the heart of Cheshire, past an ancient mill set in a sleepy hollow, then on to visit the space-age exhibitions and wonderful Arboretum at Jodrell Bank, where children of all ages can learn about the Earth and the solar system of which it is a part. There are also cross-country paths and quiet country lanes to meander along, making for a really rewarding excursion into the Cheshire countryside.

The Walk
On leaving the inn, turn right and then left to enter Cinder Lane. Pass the tiny red-brick building of Over Peover Methodist church and, on meeting a junction of lanes, keep forward where a sign points towards 'Bate Mill'. Descend, pass under a railway bridge and follow the lane as it turns to the right. On the left is a small reservoir which provides a head of water for Bate Mill. The building on the right contains the water wheel, which is of the undershot type. Records show that a mill has stood on this site for centuries.

Leave the lane via a stile on the left and walk along the side of the reservoir. After 50 metres, go over a footbridge on the right and climb up the left-hand edge of a rough field, keeping a fence and trees on your immediate left. Go over a stile at the field corner and continue along the edge of the next two fields, crossing two stiles along the way. Emerge onto a lane and turn right to pass the head of Batemill Lane, which goes

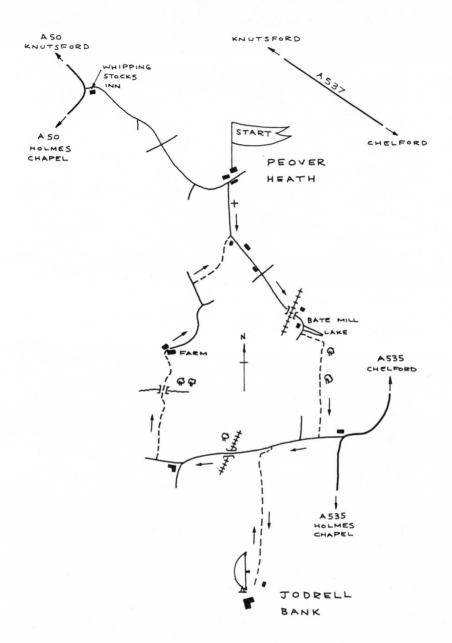

A 50
KNUTSFORD

WHIPPING
STOCKS
INN

A 50
HOLMES
CHAPEL

KNUTSFORD

A 537

CHELFORD

START

PEOVER
HEATH

BATE MILL
LAKE

A 535
CHELFORD

FARM

N

A 535
HOLMES
CHAPEL

JODRELL
BANK

off to the right. Over to the left the giant dish of the radio telescope at Jodrell Bank comes into view. A few more metres and you arrive at the entrance drive to Jodrell Bank Science Centre and Arboretum. If you want to visit the site, turn left to reach the admission kiosk. Time spent here is most rewarding. There is an Environmental Discovery Centre, an Arboretum and a Science Centre, complete with Planetarium.

The Environmental Discovery Centre is located on the edge of the Arboretum, where over 2,500 varieties of trees occupy a 35 acre site. Here the visitor can wander freely, study the trees, observe the wildlife, admire the flowers and take a look at pond life. An illustrated map is available which outlines a number of different trails through the site.

In the shade of the giant telescope is the Science Centre – which is a mecca for all those interested in space. There are many exhibits, a number of which are interactive, thus encouraging the visitor to learn through direct experience. The general admittance ticket gives access to one of the shows in the Planetarium, which are usually held at 45 minute intervals throughout the day.

Jodrell Bank is open from the third weekend in March to the last weekend in October, daily from 10.30 am to 5.30 pm. During winter weekends and Christmas holidays (except Christmas Day) the site is open from 11 am to 4.30 pm. The last admission to the Planetarium is one hour before closing. The site telephone number is: 01477 571339.

On completion of the visit, retrace your steps back along the entrance drive to arrive at the crossing lane. Turn left and follow the lane, which quickly passes over the railway. Shortly, the lane turns to the left, but keep right here to enter a narrow lane which commences at the right-hand side of a dwelling. After only 150 metres, leave the lane over a stile on the right which is at the side of a field gate. Follow the facing field edge, keeping a fence, then a hedgerow, on your immediate right. Go through a gate at the field corner and descend along a rough track. Cross a bridge which takes you over a stream, go through a facing gate, and climb along a track. On reaching the top of the climb, bear right and pass in front of a farmhouse. A tablet set into the frontage tells you that the building was constructed in 1762 by John and Ann Wright.

Follow a narrow macadam lane which takes you away from the farm. The lane passes a bungalow, then winds, and leads to a crossing lane. Turn left and after 200 metres leave the lane over a stile on the right where a footpath sign points across a field. Keep along the right-hand edge of the field. At the field corner, and close by a dwelling, pass over two stiles in quick succession. After a further 50 metres enter a lane over a stile at the side of a field gate. Turn left along the lane. Pass the Methodist church and, at the junction ahead, turn right to arrive back at the inn.

11 Gawsworth
The Harrington Arms

Although its beautiful hall and ancient church are the pride of the village, Gawsworth possesses many more architectural attractions. There is the New Hall, founded by Lord Mohun; the Old Post Office – the oldest shop in the village; and the White House, which once served as the village school.

Reputed to be over 400 years old, and still part of a working farm, the Harrington Arms is a friendly pub, full of character. The premises belong to the Robinson Brewery of Stockport, hence Robinson's Best Mild and Best Bitter are both available, together with various lagers. A full range of soft drinks can also be purchased. Sandwiches, pies and other snacks are made daily and, if the weather is fine, these can be consumed at the front of the premises where there are picnic tables and seats. Food is available throughout opening hours and can be prepared to order if you ring in advance of your arrival. There are several small, wood-panelled rooms and an old oak bar and children are welcome in the family room during the daytime.

The premises are open on Monday to Saturday from 12 noon to 3 pm and in the evening from 6 pm to 11 pm. On Sunday the opening times are 12 noon to 3 pm and 7 pm to 10.30 pm.

Telephone: 01260 223325.

How to get there: Gawsworth is situated 3 miles to the south-west of Macclesfield, just off the A536 Macclesfield to Congleton road.

Parking: There is a small car park at the front of the Harrington Arms. If this is full, the farmyard at the rear may be used (please check with the landlord). Alternatively, there is a parking layby close to a telephone kiosk a little to the south-west, headed by a 'no-through-road' sign. This layby gives access to Holly Cottage, High Lane House and Gandysbrook Farm. There is also a large car park, which is specifically for visitors to Gawsworth Hall, a short distance from the Hall's main entrance.

Length of the walk: 3 miles. Map: OS Landranger 118 Stoke-on-Trent and Macclesfield (inn GR 887695).

A truly delightful place, Gawsworth is set in a beautiful part of Cheshire, between the eastern hills and the Cheshire Plain. There are really two attractions to visit on this walk, for, apart from Gawsworth Hall and Gardens, there is the splendid church of St James, whose origins go back to Norman times. Having visited the church and Hall, the walk takes you on a circular route along field paths and lanes, before returning to the Harrington Arms.

The Walk

On leaving the inn, turn left and enter Church Lane. Walk along the laneside footpath in the direction of Gawsworth church. After 250 metres, climb facing steps at the side of the rectory to enter the church confines. Some time should be spent looking in and around this fine old building (services permitting). The walls and the roof are over 500 years old, and the church stands on the site of a Norman chapel. The tombs and effigies of four generations of the Fitton family can be seen inside, the oldest of which dates from 1608. A leaflet describing points of interest for visitors is available inside the church.

Leave the church on the north side and pass between two lakes, then go through a lychgate to join a lane. Turn right, then look across to the right where Gawsworth Hall can be seen across the lake – this view being at its best in early summer when the rhododendrons and lakeside iris are in full bloom.

Turn next right (the car park for visitors to Gawsworth Hall is on the left here) and enter the entrance lane to the Hall. There are lakes on both sides here. Arrive at the entrance to the Hall and Gardens.

Although the origins of the present Hall date back to the second half of the 15th century, it is still very much a family house, for it is full of warmth and charm. About 1700 much of the original timber framing

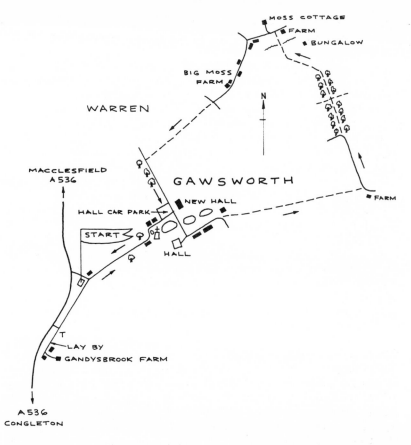

was covered with brick and this has produced an extremely interesting façade. Internally, every room presents something of note, but the long hall is the highlight.

In the gardens there is an ancient site known as a 'Tilting Ground', which covers an area of 15 acres where knights could practise their jousting skills. The gardens are completely surrounded by a brick wall which was constructed during Tudor times and this provided an enclosure for tournaments. During more recent times, in the summer the gardens have been used for outdoor theatre, especially Shakespearean productions. Regarding Shakespeare, it is said that the 'Dark Lady' of his sonnets is based on a certain Mary Fitton, who once lived in the Hall. It has been suggested that Shakespeare may have visited Gawsworth when he was journeying to the north.

Gawsworth Hall and Gardens are open to the public from late March to early October from 2 pm to 5 pm daily. Telephone for information: 01260 223456.

On leaving the Hall and Gardens turn right, pass a larger than life statue of Peel, and continue past charming mews cottages. Shortly after passing Gawsworth Court, the lane turns right – but keep straight ahead along a short section of track. Go over a stile at the side of a field gate, close by the entrance to a dwelling called The Pidgeon House, a tall, square building which sits on top of a rise on the left.

Walk forward, keeping a hedgerow on your immediate right, and cross four fields, via stiles and gates, to emerge onto a crossing lane. Turn left. After 250 metres, the lane turns sharply to the left. Leave it here and enter a facing, hedged-in path. The path takes you between tree-lined embankments. At a crossing path go forward over a facing stile and continue in the same direction as before. The path is still hedged in but, after a further 100 metres, emerge into a field over a stile.

Navigational skill is required at this point. Bear diagonally left and walk across the field to pass under electricity cables. After about 50 metres, arrive close to a hawthorn tree which forms the corner of a fence. Walk forward now, keeping the fence on your immediate right and, after 100 metres, cross a gully and a stream. Having negotiated the gully, continue in the same general direction as before, to cross a facing field. Go over a stile which is about 50 metres to the left of a small farm, and turn left to join a lane which takes you past the entrance drive of Moss Cottage. Continue along the lane and shortly arrive at a junction, where the way is left past The Dene and other houses.

This most pleasant lane takes you past a mixture of dwellings, both old and new. Pass Chestnut Cottage with its ornate coat of arms, and continue to where, about 200 metres after Big Moss Farm, you arrive at a junction of lanes. Leave the lane at this point and go over a facing stile to enter a small field. Proceed, keeping a hedgerow on your immediate right, then go over a stile at the field corner. You have now entered a long and undulating field. Walk forward along the field edge, keeping a fence on your immediate left.

There is a splendid view across the fields towards Gawsworth church, whilst over to the right can be seen the modern dwellings of the hamlet of Warren.

On reaching the end of the field, climb over a ladder-stile to arrive at a crossing lane. Turn left and follow the laneside footpath. On passing the entrance drive to the splendidly renovated Gawsworth New Hall, turn right.

You are now back on part of your initial route. Follow the lane as it winds past the church and continue back to the Harrington Arms.

12 Willington
The Boot

Willington sprawls across the lower folds of the valleys which come down from the sandstone ridge that runs across Cheshire from Helsby to Beeston. The village is close to the Roman Watling Street which linked the salt towns with the garrison at Chester. Its history stretches further back than Roman times, for there are the remains of a Bronze Age castle on nearby Kelsborrow Hill.

A very attractive country pub, the Boot was once a row of small cottages nestling close to the hills of the Central Cheshire Sandstone Ridge. Stone floors, low ceilings and real fires on cold days produce an ambience seemingly untouched by time. The premises offer all the qualities you would expect to find in a traditional English pub – including a warm welcome – and individuals and families alike are made to feel at home. A beer garden and patio area with trestle tables and benches provide outside seating for use in fine weather.

Real ales in the form of a selection of guest beers from all over the country can be sampled, together with some fine wines, and there is a wide variety of superb home-cooked food available that can be eaten in the bar or in the inn's charming restaurant. Appetisers include home-made pâté, hot garlic prawns, warm smoked trout, glazed black pudding and garlic bread, as well as the more traditional soup of the day. The tempting main courses are just as comprehensive – beef and ale pie, traditional Cumberland sausage, lamb tikka masala, scampi, plaice, Basque-style bake, liver and bacon casserole, gammon and pineapple, and a variety of steaks. Vegetarian dishes are available and there is a range of 'Cold Platters' and sandwiches. A selection of home-made sweets and liqueur coffees is also on offer. A 'Daily Specials' blackboard expands the menu even further.

Food is available at lunchtimes between 11 am and 2.30 pm on Monday to Saturday, and on Sunday from 12 noon to 2.30 pm. During the evening food is served between 6 pm and 9.30 pm on Monday to Saturday and between 7 pm and 9.30 pm every Sunday.

Telephone: 01829 751375.

How to get there: The village of Kelsall nestles in hilly country 7 miles due east of Chester. In days gone by the bulk of the village straddled the busy A54 road; however, a new bypass has eased traffic flow. One mile to the south of Kelsall is the hamlet of Willington, where a short drive along Boothsdale leads to the Boot.

Parking: There is a large car park in front of the Boot. Alternatively, at those times when the gardens are open to the public, parking is available within the grounds of Tirley Garth.

Length of the walk: 4 miles. Map: OS Landranger 117 Chester (inn GR 531672).

A combination of paths, tracks and lanes, plus a visit to the enchanting house and gardens at Tirley Garth, make for a most enjoyable excursion. The walk also provides, via a couple of short climbs, an opportunity to take in some long vistas across miles of rolling Cheshire countryside.

The Walk
With the inn at your back, turn left to follow a narrow, hedged-in lane. After 100 metres, there is a junction of ways. To the left is a private road, but continue ahead here to enter a sandy track between hedges, where a footpath sign points to 'Gooseberry Lane'. After only 30 metres, there is a field gate on the right, but keep forward to enter a narrow, hedged-in path. Emerge onto Gooseberry Lane opposite a dwelling called Rose Cottage. Turn right and gradually descend along the lane.

Can you spot the dwelling where the date stone has been put in upside down? (It can't have been built in 1061, can it?)

At the junction of lanes turn left to climb up a lane called Rough Low. This takes you through trees and on past Roughlow Farm and Summer

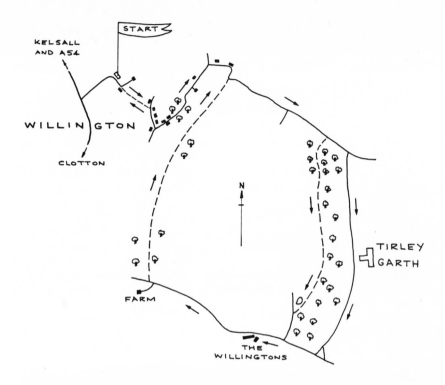

Bank. Pass Waste Lane, which goes off to the left, and continue past a large dwelling on the left which has a sundial set into its facing wall. The going is flat and level now. Follow the lane as it turns to the right. There is a dwelling on the left here, called Summertrees, where light refreshments are served during the summer months.

Continue along the lane and pass a hedged-in track which goes off to the right (Sandstone Trail). The next section of lane provides a platform for some marvellous long vistas. Keep on past a hedged-in lane which goes off to the right and arrive at a footpath which begins through a gate on the right, where a sign indicates 'John Street'.

If you are visiting Tirley Garth continue for a further 30 metres to arrive at the entrance to the formal gardens. If you are not visiting Tirley Garth, or if the gardens are closed, you must take the footpath to John Street. To do this, leave the lane, pass through a gate, and follow a well-defined path which descends through trees. The path hugs the right-hand side of Tirley Garth estate and it must be remembered that the grounds to your left are private property – so please keep to the path. The path descends and allows glimpses of the house through the

59

trees on the left. Go through a gate and pass close to a pond, on your right, emerging onto a lane through a gate. Turn left and after 60 metres arrive at a crossing lane, where the way is right (which is the joining place of the route if Tirley Garth has been visited).

Time spent at Tirley Garth is most rewarding. As you meander down the entrance drive during May and June there is an abundance of colour from the rhododendrons and azaleas which line the drive and adorn the lawns of this magnificent 40 acre estate. At the centre is an impressive house, built as a gentleman's residence during Edwardian times and developed by Richard Prestwich – a Manchester businessman who spent a considerable amount of his fortune on the estate.

From the house you can look out across the village of nearby Utkinton, towards the castles of Beeston and Peckforton, or westwards towards the mountains of Wales.

Although only open to the public on a limited number of days each year (mainly Sundays during late May and early June) the estate is a venue for a wide variety of different events, including talks, concerts and conferences. Souvenirs, guidebooks and refreshments can be purchased – whilst video shows relate the history and development of the property. For more information write to: Friends of Tirley Garth, Tirley Garth, Tarporley, Cheshire CW6 0LZ. Telephone: 01829 732301.

On leaving the house, continue along the gently descending drive and arrive at a crossing lane, where the way is right. Keep on past a narrow lane which goes off to the right (which is the joining place of the route which has to be used when Tirley Garth is closed).

The lane takes you past a large farm called The Willingtons. After almost $1/2$ mile there is the entrance to a farm on the left, and 15 metres further on, on the right, there is a sandy, hedged-in track which climbs away from the lane. A sign here indicates 'Delamere' and shows that you are walking along the Sandstone Trail, one of Cheshire's long-distance footpaths. Follow the track as it climbs away from the lane.

Near the top of the climb there are long views across to the left – where, if the day is clear, the mountains of Wales can be seen.

Emerge from the track at a crossing lane. Turn left and follow the lane as it turns to the left. You are now back on part of your initial route. Descend along the lane. Pass Waste Lane, which goes off to the right, and continue past Summer Bank and Roughlow Farm. Arrive at Gooseberry Lane – which goes off to the right.

Enter Gooseberry Lane and climb to where the hedged-in path begins opposite Rose Cottage. A sign here indicates 'Boothsdale'. On emerging from the hedged-in path follow the facing macadam lane to arrive back at the Boot and the car.

13 Chester
The Boathouse

Chester has a rich architectural heritage where a mixture of 17th-century dwellings, with mainly Victorian black and white façades, blend with stately Georgian houses which form a backdrop to the imposing building of the cathedral. There are also traces of the Roman occupation and a virtually complete circuit of city walls. During the Middle Ages, vessels from all over Europe sailed up the river Dee to trade at the port of Chester and a fine sandstone bridge survives from this period. Today, the waters of the Dee are mainly used by pleasure craft which can be hired from a riverside promenade.

The Boathouse, as its name implies, was once used to store rivercraft. Built during the 17th century, the pub has two separate buildings – one right by the river. The Riverside Bar overlooks the Dee, which is always a source of interest with its varied river traffic, whilst the Aletaster Bar is a few metres away.

There is a good choice of liquid refreshment, with three to four guest ales per week and a wide selection of bottled beers, lagers, ciders and soft drinks. Food is served every lunchtime and there are many dishes to tempt the tastebuds. The starters include home-made soup, home-made pâté and garlic mushrooms. Main courses consist of deep-fried cod, breast of chicken, steak and kidney pie, gammon, lasagne, chilli, and a cross-section of Yorkshire puddings with different fillings. Jacket potatoes, sandwiches and hot baguettes can also be purchased. Different sweets are available daily and the beverages include tea, coffee and hot chocolate. There is also a comprehensive wine list. Children are very welcome and have their own menu. Accommodation includes a family room, a no-smoking area and a large outside patio area close by the riverside.

Food is served every lunchtime between 11.30 am and 3 pm on Monday to Saturday and between 12 noon and 3.30 pm on Sunday but not in the evenings.

Telephone: 01244 328709.

How to get there: The A51 Nantwich to Chester road enters the city of Chester on the eastern side in an area called Broughton. From the A51 enter Dee Lane, which commences opposite a pub called City Tavern. A sign at the head of Dee Lane points to 'River Dee and The Groves'. On reaching the bottom of Dee Lane bear right to arrive close by the river and the Boathouse.

Parking: There is a large car park at the inn. There are numerous alternative parking places, although, at peak periods, these are at a premium.

Length of the walk: 2 miles. Map: OS Landranger 117 Chester (inn GR 412661).

There is so much to see on this walk that its attraction is best described as 'The City of Chester' – where 2,000 years of history have produced a legacy of Roman remains, a virtually complete circuit of medieval walls, 17th-century, timber-framed houses and a cathedral and churches to rival any in England. Combine all these attractions with a picturesque riverside walk and you have the ingredients for a most fulfilling stroll.

The Walk

Ask any ten people to describe their favourite walk through the city of Chester and you will probably be presented with ten different routes. There is so much to see and virtually every street and passageway leads to an interesting location. Hence, the described route can be adhered to in total or varied to suit individual taste. It is impossible to get lost for you can always make your way back to the riverside and the inn.

On leaving the inn, follow the riverside promenade and cross a large suspension footbridge which traverses the river. The bridge, which was originally constructed in 1852 but rebuilt in 1923, is an elegant piece of

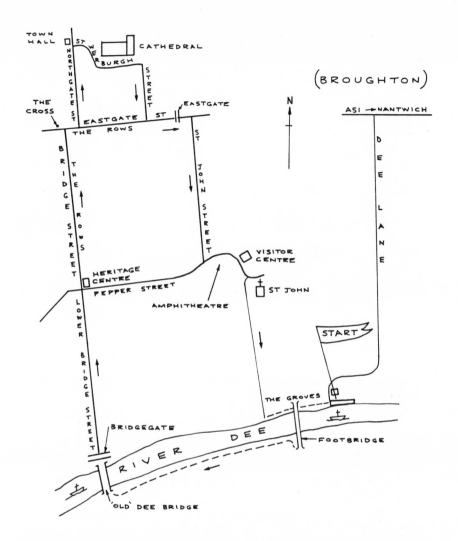

engineering design and connects The Groves with Queen's Park on the opposite bank.

Having crossed the bridge, turn right and descend to a riverside path where the way is left. Follow the lower path (the one nearest to the river) and pass close to a restored water wheel. A weir stretches out diagonally across the river at this point. Walk under the overhanging extensions of a couple of blocks of flats and arrive at the 'Old' Dee Bridge. This is probably Roman in origin although the structure that we

63

The river Dee at Chester.

see today dates from the 14th century. Up to the 19th century it was the only bridge crossing the river to give access to the city.

Go across the bridge and pass under Bridgegate. This gate, medieval in origin, guarded the approach to Chester from North Wales. The present arch was built by Chester Corporation in 1782.

Straight ahead is Lower Bridge Street, which is rich in architectural splendour. On the left is the Bear and Billet Hotel, a fine example of a 17th-century, black-and-white timber building. Opposite are splendid Georgian houses – one of which is owned by Granada TV News. Continue past Duke Street and gradually climb. The buildings are a mixture of ancient and modern.

On reaching the junction with Pepper Street, arrive at the Heritage Centre, housed in what was St Michael's church. The first of its type, it was opened during 1975 to commemorate European Architectural Heritage Year and contains displays relating to many aspects of Chester's architecture. There is information about the use of local materials, listed buildings, conservation and the finances of restoration. A video display, coupled with a taped commentary, projects a graphic picture of Chester throughout its long and varied history. The Centre is open on Monday to Saturday from 11 am to 5 pm and on Sunday from 12 noon to 5 pm (closed 24th and 25th December, 1st January and Good Friday). Telephone: 01244 317948.

When you leave the Heritage Centre, continue in the same direction as before, along Bridge Street Rows. The 'Rows' are two tiers of shops where the top tier is protected by an overhang which forms a protective balcony. Again, there are numerous interesting shops and businesses to explore. On reaching the junction with Watergate Street, 'The Cross' can be seen down on the left, standing at the junction of Chester's four principal streets. It was smashed during the Civil War (1642–49) but the pieces were preserved and it was restored and placed in its original position during 1975, a position it had previously occupied since 1407.

Leave the Rows here and enter Northgate Street, which commences at the side of St Peter's church (founded AD 907). A short stroll takes you to the interesting cathedral and its environs. Standing on the site of a Saxon church, the present building dates from the 11th century. Previously an abbey, it became the cathedral of the See of Chester in 1541, and has remained so ever since.

On leaving the cathedral, walk along St Werburgh Street to arrive at Eastgate Street, where the way is left, to pass under the Eastgate, with its ornate clock – which was installed to commemorate the diamond jubilee of Queen Victoria. Turn next right to enter St John Street. Pass the Blossoms Hotel and the Wesley Methodist church to arrive at a junction. Opposite is the site of one of the largest Roman amphitheatres yet discovered in Britain. Turn left and arrive at Chester Visitor Centre.

The Visitor Centre, where the admission is free, puts on video presentations, has a Victorian street exhibition, provides souvenirs and offers refreshments and general information relating to the city of Chester.

From the Centre, cross the road and pass to the right of the parish church of St John the Baptist. Keep on, past the sandstone remains of an earlier church, to follow a narrow path between walls. The path descends down steps and leads to the riverside, and an area where boats can be hired.

Turn left, and pass under the large suspension footbridge which you crossed earlier in the walk, to arrive back at the Boathouse and the car.

14 Tattenhall
The Poacher's Pocket

Tattenhall is in the midst of some lush green, Cheshire countryside. The reason for this abundance is no doubt due to the prolific number of waterways within the area. There is the river Gowy, the Golbourne Brook, the Mere Brook, Crimes Brook and the Shropshire Union Canal – all of which have links with the mighty river Mersey.

Situated in the heart of the Cheshire Plain, the Poacher's Pocket is a converted, 18th-century farmhouse where generous portions of good, honest food are served in pleasant surroundings at modest prices. The inn has an attractive interior and meals can be eaten in a number of raised alcoves which lead off from the main bar area. Accommodation includes a no-smoking area and a beer garden, and children are made very welcome.

The poacher's theme is carried through the menu with Poacher's 14 oz giant rump steak, Bailiff's big 16 oz gammon steak, Stalker's steak and kidney pie, special Poacher's meaty mixed grill, Beater's 8 oz sirloin steak and various other assorted dishes. For those with a really huge appetite there is the Poacher's Challenge, which consists of a 28 oz roast turkey drumstick accompanied by a 24 oz chicken and bacon pie all served with a special Gamekeeper's gravy – together with a free pint of Banks's ale. As well as the main menu, there is also a selection of daily specials, together with a wide range of puddings – including delicious whipped ice cream sundaes. On Sundays a good-value traditional roast lunch is on offer. To complement the food there is a range of Banks's ales, draught cider and a wide selection of soft drinks.

Meals are served every day at lunchtime between 12 noon and 2 pm on Monday to Friday and between 12 noon and 2.30 pm on Saturday and Sunday. In the evening food is available between 5.30 pm and 10 pm on Monday to Saturday and between 7 pm and 9 pm on Sunday.

Telephone: 01829 771010.

How to get there: The A41 connects Chester with Whitchurch. Tattenhall is about 1 mile to the east of this road and about 3 miles to the north of its junction with the A534. The Poacher's Pocket is 1 mile to the north of Tattenhall, in the direction of Huxley, and close to where the road bridges the railway and the Shropshire Union Canal.

Parking: There is a car park at the side of the Poacher's Pocket. There is also a car park, which is specifically for visitors, at Cheshire Ice Cream Farm.

Length of the walk: 3 miles. Map: OS Landranger 117 Chester (inn GR 492602).

The Cheshire Ice Cream Farm.

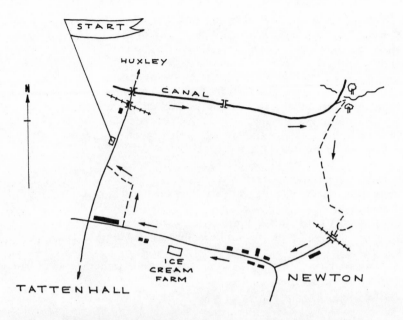

Close to the twin castles of Beeston and Peckforton lies one of Cheshire's more unusual tourist attractions – Cheshire Ice Cream Farm, where 30 different flavours of ice creams and sorbets can be sampled. A visit to the farm, coupled with a short circular walk from the Poacher's Pocket, taking in a stretch of the Shropshire Union Canal, results in an interesting and varied excursion.

The Walk

On leaving the Poacher's Pocket, turn left and follow the road over the railway. After a further 150 metres, leave the road, to the right, just before the canal bridge, and walk along the towpath of the Shropshire Union Canal.

The twin castles of Beeston and Peckforton can be seen on the skyline straight ahead – one a medieval ruin, the other a 19th-century folly.

Pass under a bridge and continue along the towpath. The canal gently bends to the left shortly and care is required in order not to miss the point at which you leave the towpath. Where the canal is raised above the surrounding fields, a stream can be seen down on the right, flowing at right angles to the canal. Leave the towpath here and descend to pass over an iron fence-stile, then turn right to join a path which leads from a tunnel under the canal. After 60 metres there is a facing metal field gate and to its left a wooden gate. However, the way is to the right over a stile which gives access to a large field.

Follow the field edge, keeping a hedgerow on your immediate right at first. After 150 metres, there is a gap in the hedge on the right, where there is also a circular water tank. At this point bear diagonally left to cross the field. An approximate guiding point is a tall, individual, evergreen tree which can be seen across the field about 300 metres away. Join a track near the field corner and turn left to go over a stile at the right-hand side of a facing metal gate. Continue along the track, which quickly turns to the right. At a junction of tracks turn right and pass under a bridge which carries the railway overhead.

The way is now along a facing macadam lane, which leads past a row of cottages. Arrive at a junction of lanes and turn right. Pass Ford Farm, Rose Cottage, Yew Tree Farm and Newton Lodge. Pass other dwellings and after a further 250 metres arrive at Cheshire Ice Cream Farm.

A visit to the premises provides an opportunity to obtain an inside view of how ice cream is made, together with a mouth-watering chance to enjoy some of the many varieties. The actual manufacturing process takes about 24 hours and on weekdays you may be able to observe the final freezing and packing stages through the dairy windows. Most unusually, you can sample as many as you like, including sorbets and liqueur ice creams – absolutely free! Apart from the ice cream you can take a first-hand look at life on the farm, where you can see the calves bred from the herd. There is also Caroline's Pantry, where a range of home-made snacks can be eaten in surroundings reminiscent of a real farmhouse kitchen.

Cheshire Ice Cream Farm is open between 10 am and 5.30 pm from April to October and between 10.30 am and 5 pm from November to March, seven days a week, including bank holidays (except Christmas and New Year). The premises are closed the last week in January and the first week in February. Telephone for information: 01829 770995.

On leaving the farm turn left and continue along the lane. Pass a couple of dwellings and then arrive at a row of houses on the right. Do not walk past these houses but turn right to pass over a stile at the side of a field gate just before them. Enter a field and walk forward, keeping the garden fence of the first house on your immediate left. Where the fence finishes, keep forward and walk straight across the facing field. About 30 metres before arriving at a crossing hedgerow, turn left and gradually converge with the hedge to arrive at the field corner where a stile takes you onto a crossing lane.

Turn right and after a few more strides arrive back at the Poacher's Pocket and the car.

15 Scholar Green
The Rising Sun

The district around Scholar Green is known as Odd Rode and is made up of several small villages in the shadow of Mow Cop. An elevated section of the Macclesfield Canal cuts through the area and provides a platform for long views across the Cheshire Plain.

The Rising Sun is a local village freehouse which has, during recent years, been extensively renovated – resulting in a hostelry of charm and character. Three cottages were joined together to make the original inn, becoming an establishment where both locals and travellers from the adjacent Macclesfield Canal could obtain sustenance. Internally, there are a number of quiet corners in which to relax, together with an extended dining room.

The inn serves a range of Marston's, Robinson's and Tetley beers, together with draught cider. Weekly guest beers are also on offer. The catering facilities provide a comprehensive selection of meals, both at lunchtime and during the evening. Traditional Sunday lunches are a speciality. All dishes are freshly prepared and home-cooked, using fresh local produce when available. The extensive blackboard-style menu is frequently changed and visitors would be hard pressed not to discover dishes which suited their tastes. Accompanied children are

made welcome in the dining room up to 8 pm in the evening. The opening hours are 12 noon to 3 pm and 7 pm to 11 pm (10.30 pm on Sunday). Food is available from 12 noon to 2 pm (2.30 pm on Sunday) and 7 pm to 9.30 pm.
Telephone: 01782 776235.

How to get there: The bulk of the village of Scholar Green lies to the east of the A34, midway between Congleton and Newcastle-under-Lyme, about 1 mile to the north of the junction between the A34 and the A50. The Rising Sun is about ½ mile from the A34, in the direction of Mow Cop, close to where Station Road crosses the Macclesfield Canal.

Parking: There is a car park at the rear of the Rising Sun. Alternatively, there is a parking layby on Station Road between the A34 and the inn. There is also a large car park, which is specifically for visitors, at Little Moreton Hall.

Length of the walk: 3 miles. Map: OS Landranger 118 Stoke-on-Trent and Macclesfield (inn GR 837575).

It is often apparent that our aristocratic ancestors knew exactly what they were about when choosing a site for their manor houses. Little Moreton Hall is typical, being sited in a lovely vale and protected from the elements by the hill of Mow Cop. The circular walk can be extended to this black-and-white masterpiece in its idyllic location, and also takes in a picturesque section of the Macclesfield Canal, as well as field paths, lanes and tracks through a peaceful area of rural Cheshire.

The Walk
On leaving the inn, cross the road and turn left to walk along the roadside pavement. Pass Cinderhill Lane, which goes off to the left, and then turn right to enter a hedged-in lane, which takes you between fields. After ¼ mile, the lane bends to the left and leads towards a large farm. Leave it here, over a stile on the right, to follow a path which skirts the edge of a wood that is on the left. Gradually climb and then emerge onto the towpath of the Macclesfield Canal, over a stile. Turn left and walk along the towpath.

Shortly, over to the right, can be seen the splendid three-storey brick building of Ramsdell Hall, which was built during the 18th century.

Approach a stone bridge which traverses the canal. Do not walk under this bridge, but go over a stile on the left where a sign indicates 'Little Moreton Hall'. Join a track which leads away from the bridge and pass through a gate. The track takes you to a stile at the side of a gate. Cross the stile and turn right to follow the edge of a large field, keeping a

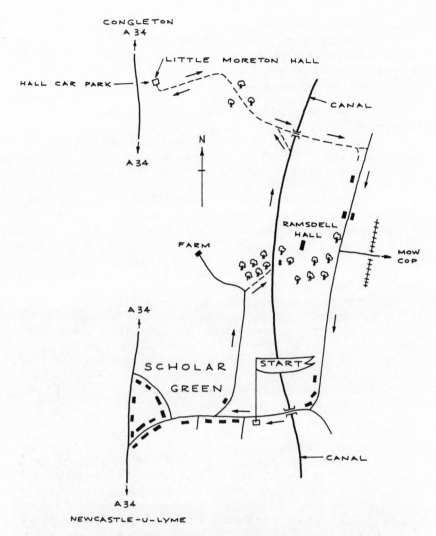

hedgerow on your immediate right. At the field corner, go over a stile and follow the edge of the next field. On crossing a stile at the side of a facing gate, bear diagonally left, and walk towards farm buildings which can be seen about 300 metres away. On converging with a hedgerow on the right, go over a stile in a crossing fence. Pass along a field edge in front of the farmhouse and outbuildings, then go over a stile at the field corner. Walk along a facing driveway and then turn right to arrive at the magnificent black-and-white building of Little Moreton Hall.

The moated Hall, which was the ancestral home of the Moreton family until acquired by the National Trust in 1937, has been little altered since it was constructed during the late 15th and early 16th centuries. Because the family became financially strained (due to their participation in the English Civil War), they had very little money to spare for alterations to the property. Luckily, their deprivation has resulted in the unaltered survival of one of the finest examples of half-timber work in the country.

The Hall is timber-framed throughout its construction, apart from the sturdy brick chimney-breasts and a small amount of additional, brick strengthening here and there. Externally, the building has many carved gables and ornate windows, whilst internally there is impressive panelling, furniture and pewter. Unlike Gawsworth Hall (walk 11), it is a museum rather than a home, although this does not detract from its appeal. It is claimed by many to be the most popular of all English black-and-white houses, a boast supported by the numerous calendars in which it appears.

The Hall is open to the public from late March to the end of September, every afternoon except Tuesday (closed Good Friday). Telephone for information: 01260 272018.

On leaving the Hall, retrace the route back to the Macclesfield Canal.

The Elizabethan splendour of Little Moreton Hall.

73

On this section of the walk there are long views ahead to the well known folly at Mow Cop, which sits on top of the facing hill.

Instead of rejoining the canal towpath, follow the facing track and cross the canal via the stone bridge. Go through a gate and continue on the track as it leads away from the bridge. Shortly, the track turns to the right, but keep forward here and go over a stile at the side of a gate. Enter a lane, turn right and follow the laneside pavement.

Pass the splendid Georgian dwelling of Old House Green and continue past The Coach House and Old House Green Cottage, to arrive at the magnificent entrance gates to Ramsdell Hall. A road on the left here goes off to Mow Cop – but keep forward along the laneside pavement in the direction of Scholar Green.

Continue past the Heritage Narrow Boat Marina and then bear right to pass over the canal via a sturdy stone bridge. A few more strides and you are back at the Rising Sun and the car.

16 Bunbury
The Yew Tree

The village of Bunbury, which is dominated by a very beautiful church, lies in rich farming country to the east of the Central Cheshire Sandstone Ridge.

Built by Lord Crewe during the early part of the 19th century, the inn was enlarged during 1994. The extension was tastefully carried out and the original character maintained, with oak beams and open fireplaces to complement the original fixtures and fittings.

Ales from Burtonwood Brewery and Boddingtons are served, together with draught Strongbow cider. The inn specialises in 'food with a difference' and the offerings include game, steaks, fresh fish and Scottish Highland dishes, as well as a wide selection of more conventional fare. A daily blackboard proclaims additional choices. The Yew Tree has a family room, a no-smoking section, a beer garden and a children's play area outside. Accompanied children are welcome to enjoy food inside.

Meals are served every lunchtime between 12 noon and 2 pm and in the evening between 7 pm and 9.30 pm.

Telephone: 01829 260274.

How to get there: The A49 bypasses Tarporley and heads south towards Whitchurch. About 4 miles to the south of Tarporley is the hamlet of Spurstow, where there are crossroads. Enter Long Lane Spurstow and drive in the direction of Bunbury and Haughton. After only ¼ mile, arrive at the Yew Tree Inn, which is at the junction with Bunbury Lane.

Parking: There is a car park at the inn. Alternatively, there is a roadside parking area near Bunbury church, close to where a footpath leads to Bunbury Water Mill. Also, there is a small car park at the mill.

Length of the walk: 3 miles. Map: OS Landranger 117 Chester (inn GR 563572).

Apart from the visit to Bunbury Water Mill, there is the added attraction on this walk of a visit to a very beautiful medieval church, the origins of which date back to the 8th century AD. The village of Bunbury is also a delight, and contains many interesting half-timbered cottages. The walk takes in tracks, field paths and virtually traffic-free country lanes through a rich and fertile farming community.

The Walk
On leaving the inn, enter Bunbury Lane and, after only 50 metres, turn right to enter a hedged-in track. The track finishes at a facing gate. Go through the gate and walk across a narrow field to pass through a small metal gate. Gradually converge with a hedge on the left then go through a wooden gate at the field corner. Turn sharp left now through a field gap and continue, with a hedge on your immediate right, in the direction of dwellings which can be seen straight ahead. Pass through a wooden kissing-gate close by a long, wooden building and continue along the edge of the next field. On passing through another gate, a short stretch of path takes you close to dwellings and leads to a crossing lane, where the way is left.

The lane narrows and leads to Wyche Road, where Bunbury church comes into view. Bear right and follow Wyche Road in the direction of the church. Down on the right can be seen a pond which is well stocked with goldfish.

Where the lane begins to descend, go over a stile on the right, opposite a dwelling called Wyndhurst. Keeping a garden hedge on your immediate left, follow the edge of a sloping field. The dwelling on your left is the Chantry House and dates from 1527. It is of box-framed construction and has recently been restored.

Shortly, return to Wyche Road, via a stile, and turn right to climb up to the church, passing picturesque cottages en route. Visitors are most welcome at the church, which is dedicated to St Boniface, who died in AD 755. The church contains the alabaster tomb and effigy

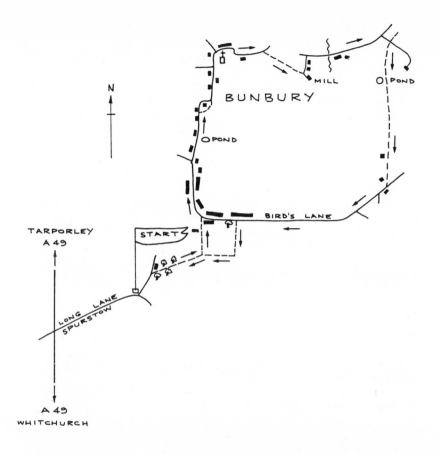

N

TARPORLEY
A 49

BUNBURY

MILL

O POND

O POND

BIRD'S LANE

START

LONG LANE
SPURSTOW

A 49
WHITCHURCH

of Sir Hugh Calveley, who rendered great service to the Black Prince. Sir Hugh instigated the 14th-century remodelling of the building and established it as a collegiate church. In 1940, it was hit by a landmine and its roof, windows and half of one side were blown out. Thankfully, the main structure remained intact and all the damaged areas were restored. The church is overlooked by the Dysart Arms and other tall-chimneyed dwellings.

Leave the church confines at the rear and walk past Bunbury Medical Practice. After a further 60 metres, go over a stile which takes you into a large field. At the far side of the field can be seen three, separate, brick buildings. Walk in the direction of the low building on the right and, on meeting a crossing hedge, go over a stile at the side of a gate to arrive at Bunbury Water Mill.

There has been a mill on the site since the 17th century, although the present building dates from 1850. The mill was worked as a going concern until 1960 and then lay dormant until it was completely renovated by the North West Water Authority during 1977. The restoration involved replacing 260 beechwood gear cogs and the rotted oak drive shaft, and fitting the water wheel with new buckets made of elm. The mill pond was also cleared out and reshaped and a new flood-gate manufactured. When the mill was officially reopened, the water wheel was set in motion by a member of the family – the Parkers – who had been concerned with running the mill between 1890 and 1960.

The mill is open between 2 pm and 5 pm at weekends and on bank holidays from Easter to September. Telephone for information: 01270 665667.

Having completed your visit to the mill, leave by the approach track, passing the stile by which you arrived. Continue past a couple of dwellings to reach a crossing lane. Turn right and follow the lane, which shortly takes you over a stream. Pass a pair of picturesque black-and-white dwellings and, 100 metres further on, enter a narrow, hedged-in, driveway on the right. It may appear that this is a private drive, but it is in fact a public right of way. After 50 metres, a footpath crosses the drive. Turn right here and go over a stile to follow a path which takes you between fences and trees. A facing stile gives access to a large field. Keeping a fence and trees on your immediate right, continue to a stile in a crossing fence. Go over the stile and then pass close to a fenced-in pond. On crossing a pair of stiles linking a plank-bridge, you have entered a large field.

A dwelling can be seen about ¼ mile away, straight ahead. Walk towards the left of this, gradually moving away from the hedge on your right. Arrive at the corner of a hedgerow which forms a paddock surrounding the dwelling. Go forward here, keeping the hedgerow on your immediate right, and walk to the field corner, where a stile gives access to a lane.

Turn right and follow this narrow, macadam lane to where, after ½ mile, dwellings on the right are reached. After a further 80 metres, leave the lane, to the left, to enter a track which begins close to where a seat is set at the base of a large tree. The track takes you into a large field. There is a stile on the right here, but ignore this and turn right to follow a path, which is never too far away from the hedge on the right. At the field corner, go through a wooden gate at the left of the field gap to enter another field.

You are now back on part of your initial route. Retrace your earlier way back across the next two fields, down the hedged-in track and back to Bunbury Lane and the inn.

17 Higher Burwardsley
The Pheasant Inn

Situated midway along the Sandstone Trail, the Pheasant Inn nestles close to the top of the Peckforton Hills where there are magnificent views to the Welsh hills and across the Cheshire Plain towards Frodsham and Helsby. It is of half-timbered and sandstone construction and can claim a history going back over 300 years. Originally a farm, the farmhouse kitchen has been turned into a Bistro Restaurant and there is a large conservatory where children are made welcome. The lounge bar exudes old world charm and boasts the biggest log fire in Cheshire – a welcome sight when the weather is cool.

The inn has a well-earned reputation for its food and wines and offers a range of Bass real ales, together with frequently changed guest beers, and a well-stocked bar. A very comprehensive menu is available and amongst the specialities is Highland beef. A no-smoking section, a family room, a beer garden and a play area for children are provided and the Pheasant also offers a high standard of accommodation, making this an ideal base for visitors wishing to explore the district.

Meals are served every lunchtime between 12 noon and 2.30 pm and in the evening between 7 pm and 10 pm (9 pm on Sunday).

Telephone: 01829 770434.

How to get there: The A534 connects Nantwich with Farndon. About 4 miles from Farndon, the A41 crosses the A534 at Broxton. From this intersection and about ½ mile along the A534 in the direction of Nantwich, there is the Copper Mine pub, with a turn off to Harthill and Burwardsley a little further east. At the post office in Burwardsley there is a right turn. The Pheasant Inn is at the top of the hill.

Parking: There is a car park at the side of the inn. There is also a large car park, for visitors, at Cheshire Candle Workshops.

Length of the walk: 3 miles. Map: OS Landranger 117 Chester (inn GR 523566).

This walk amongst the Peckforton Hills takes you close to the summit of Bulkeley Hill, which is a platform for panoramic views across the plains of east Cheshire. However, because the route commences in the hill village of Higher Burwardsley, there are no strenuous climbs to undertake in reaching locations where such superb vistas can be absorbed.

The Walk

On leaving the inn, turn left, go straight over the crossroads and arrive at the Cheshire Candle Workshops.

These workshops create a range of individual, hand-carved candles and glass sculptures, and they are open every day between 10 am and 5 pm, including bank holidays. Telephone: 01829 770401.

On concluding your visit to the workshops, enter the lane by which you arrived and continue past a sign which says 'Unsuitable for Motors'. On passing a dwelling called Whittlesfield, the lane starts to go down. At the bottom of the descent continue along the lane – which is hewn out of the rock at this point. Pass Quarry Cottage (the quarry can be seen over to the left). Pass another dwelling and descend again. After 200 metres, the lane turns to the right, towards Burwardsley church, which can be seen 250 metres away. Leave the lane here, to the left, over a stile, where a footpath sign points towards the 'Sandstone Trail' and 'Rawhead'. You have entered a rough, undulating field. Walk forward, to follow a path which stays on higher ground, with a stream on your right.

Pass over a track and walk towards an electricity pole, which can be seen about 200 metres away, straight ahead. On passing this, enter woodland, over a stile and plank-bridge, to follow a well-defined path which climbs between trees and undergrowth. Emerge from the trees over a stile and enter a large, sloping field. Gradually climb along a facing path to arrive at a stile in a crossing hedgerow.

Before crossing this stile, turn around to admire long views across the Cheshire Plain towards Frodsham and the Mersey estuary.

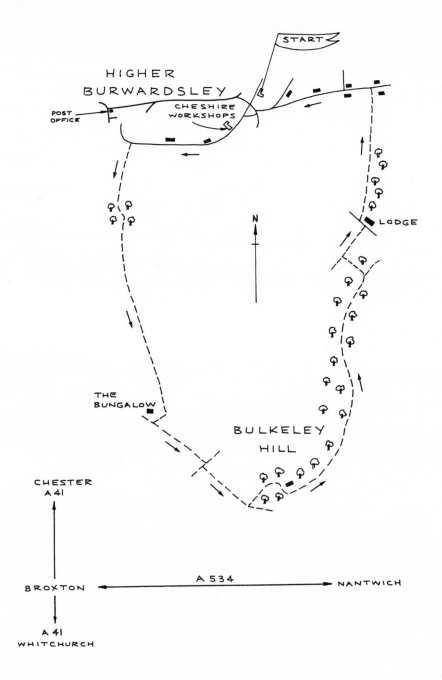

START

HIGHER
BURWARDSLEY

POST
OFFICE

CHESHIRE
WORKSHOPS

N

LODGE

THE
BUNGALOW

BULKELEY
HILL

CHESTER
A 41

BROXTON ⟷ A 534 ⟶ NANTWICH

A 41
WHITCHURCH

On crossing the stile, gradually climb along the edge of another large field, keeping a fence on your immediate right. At the field corner, go over a step-stile and turn right to walk along the edge of a level field, keeping a fence on your immediate right. A stile in a crossing fence takes you onto a track, close by a dwelling called The Bungalow. Turn left along the track and arrive at a T-junction. Enter a facing field through a gap in a crossing fence. Pass close to a telegraph pole and then go through a gate to enter a wood.

There is a junction of paths here. Keep to the left to follow a track, which gradually climbs, where there is an old metal fence on the left. You have now joined the Sandstone Trail.

The Trail is indicated by waymarkers, which show a footprint containing the letter 'S', together with a directional arrow.

The path winds past a concrete building and takes you close to the tree-lined summit of Bulkeley Hill. Pass through two gateposts (the gate has long since disappeared). It is in this vicinity that there are a couple of rock-slab vantage points giving long views towards Nantwich and beyond. A generally level, well-defined path takes you around the edge of the escarpment, which slopes steeply down to your right. Pass close to the terminus of a now defunct narrow-gauge railway track, which can be seen on the right.

Again, there are some splendid views from this section of the path. Across to the right can be seen Peckforton Point, a wooded hill where the entrance to a cave can be spotted in a rock slab in a clearing in the trees.

A well-defined, stony path descends through undergrowth and trees. Follow the Sandstone Trail as it turns to the left and descend steps to join a crossing track. Turn right to continue along this level track, where there is a stone wall on the immediate left. Arrive opposite a lodge house and turn left, then immediately right, to cross a stile which takes you into a field. Walk along the field edge, keeping a wall on your immediate right. Pass over a stile at the field corner and quickly pass over another stile to continue where the path is now fenced in on the left. Beyond another stile, the path is hemmed in by holly bushes. At the end of this length of path a stile gives access to a field.

Keep along the field edge in the same general direction as before and then go over a stile at the field corner to enter a lane. Turn left. On passing between two cottages, you come to a junction of lanes. The Sandstone Trail goes off to the right here, but keep forward along the facing lane, which descends and takes you past a farm. Continue beyond a lane which joins on the right and at the next junction turn right.

One more turn to the right takes you back to the Pheasant Inn and the car.

18 Barton
The Cock O'Barton

Situated in the pretty countryside of south-west Cheshire, the tiny village of Barton lies close to Farndon and the river Dee. Not far away there is an interesting water mill where flour has been produced since the 14th century.

The Cock O'Barton, which is a grade 2 listed building, can boast a history going back over 600 years. During the Civil War (1642–49) the building was commandeered by Cromwell's troops and its horses confiscated. In the less distant past the pub was under the control of the Shrewsbury postmaster. This accounts for its Shrewsbury postcode – for it is 30 miles from Shrewsbury – but less than 10 miles from Chester. The premises are so named because of the liking of former local villagers for cock-fighting, which was carried on in the area until long after its official abolition.

The pub has a pleasing interior, where exposed beams and brassware combine to produce a cosy atmosphere. When the weather is cold there are three log fires to warm away the chills. This is a freehouse, hence a varied selection of liquid refreshment is always on offer. Theakston Best Bitter and a 'Guest Ale of the Week' are featured, together with a wide choice of imported beers and spirits. Apart from traditional ales, there are over 200 different types of malt whisky! The range of meals is just as comprehensive and the interesting menu, which is constantly changing, should satisfy everyone in the family. There is also a daily board listing market-fresh food and the chef's home-made specialities. Although children are not allowed in the public bars they are welcome in the dining areas when accompanied by adults, and in the adjacent beer garden.

Meals are served at lunchtime every Sunday between 12 noon and 2 pm and during the evenings between 7 pm and 10 pm. The premises are closed during the day from Monday to Saturday inclusive.

Telephone: 01829 782277.

How to get there: The A534 connects Nantwich with Farndon. About 2 miles from Farndon, and midway between Farndon and the intersection between the A534 and the A41, is the village of Barton. The Cock O'Barton sits at the side of the A534, on the edge of the village.

Parking: There is a large car park at the rear of the Cock O'Barton. There is also a large car park, which is specifically for visitors, at Stretton Water Mill.

Length of the walk: 2¼ miles. Map: OS Landranger 117 Chester (inn GR 448542).

A short, but interesting, walk through the pretty countryside of south-west Cheshire, coupled with a visit to a lovely old restored water mill – an ideal way to spend a relaxing couple of hours.

The Walk

Enter the lane which begins at the side of the inn and walk away from the A534. In a little over ½ mile, arrive at the splendid three-storey, 17th-century, Stretton Lower Hall, with its laneside pond. Turn left here to enter a narrow lane, where a sign tells you that Stretton Water Mill is ¼ mile away. A short stroll takes you to the mill.

There has been a mill at Stretton since the 14th century, and during the 16th century it was a part of the Carden Estate. Initially, it was a timber-framed building under a thatched roof. During the 18th century the roof was raised and the thatch replaced with slates. The timber frame was also covered by sandstone blocks and weatherboarding. During 1777, a second water wheel was put in place and in 1819 the first wheel was enclosed by a stone surround. The original is a 'breast-shot' wheel, whilst the more recent one is an 'overshot' wheel.

The mill was in use until 1959, after which it fell into a state of disrepair. During 1975, it was restored by Cheshire County Council

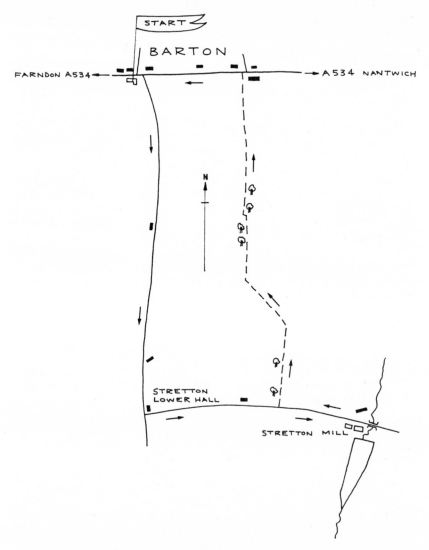

and opened the following year as a working museum. At the time of the renovation a small adjacent barn was turned into an exhibition area.

The opening times are from 1 pm to 5 pm every day except Monday, between April and the end of September (open Bank Holiday Monday afternoons). During March and October the mill is open at weekends (Saturday and Sunday only) between 1 pm and 5 pm. It is closed during the winter months. Telephone for information: 01606 41331.

The Stretton Water Mill and museum.

On leaving the mill, walk back along the lane by which you arrived. After 200 metres, and 100 metres before a dwelling on the right is reached, go over a fence stile on the right, which is at the side of a gate. Walk forward along the left-hand edge of a field, keeping a fence, hedgerow and trees on your immediate left.

Over to the right can be seen the wooded hill of Carden Cliff, which is about 1 mile away. At the field corner, go over a stile and plank-bridge to enter a large field. Bear diagonally left now, to walk to a stile which is set in a crossing hedgerow. Cross the stile and walk forward across the next field, which has a dip in the middle, and then continue, with a hedgerow on your immediate left, for 50 metres, to arrive at the field corner.

Go through a wooden gate on the left now, then turn right, and proceed along a field edge, keeping a hedgerow and trees on your immediate right. Pass through a gap at the field corner and follow a facing grassy track between a hedgerow and fence. At the end of the track go through a three-bar gate and continue. After a further 60 metres, go through a metal gate on the right and turn left to follow a hedged-in track, which takes you to a crossing road at the side of dwellings. Turn left and walk along the roadside verge. After 200 metres, arrive back at the Cock O'Barton and the car.

Cholmondeley
The Cholmondeley Arms

To the south of the Peckforton Hills, the vistas presented from the gentle wooded slopes of Cholmondeley Castle Park are a delight throughout all the seasons.

The Cholmondeley Arms was, until 1982, the village school. During 1988 the building was converted into licensed premises, when great care was taken in preserving many original architectural features in order to create a hostelry of charm and character. The high ceilings and deceptively spacious interior present a most pleasing and unusual atmosphere, where food and drink can be consumed at leisure. When the weather is fine, visitors can take their refreshment in an adjacent beer garden; conversely, when the weather is on the chilly side, real fires provide a warming glow. The adjacent School House, which forms part of the premises, provides overnight accommodation to a high standard.

The selection of drinks includes Boddingtons and Flowers IPA from the handpump, together with various lagers and ciders, and a comprehensive and well-thought-out wine list. The range of available food is extremely wide and there is something to suit every taste. Home-made soups, pâtés and pies vie with the more exotic dishes such as saffron prawns, devilled kidneys and rack of lamb grilled with Dijon mustard, garlic and herbs. A variety of starters are on offer, as well as a choice of salads and sandwiches, and the traditional ploughman's lunch. Home-made puddings are a speciality, including chocolate roulade, black cherry pavlova, hot fudged bananas, ice creams and sorbets. An array of special dishes is listed on a blackboard and there is also a special menu for children, who are always made welcome. All the food is freshly prepared and local produce is used when available.

Meals are served every day between 12 noon and 2.15 pm and in the evening from 7 pm until 10 pm.

Telephone: 01829 720300.

How to get there: The Cholmondeley Arms is situated by the A49, adjacent to the park and gardens of Cholmondeley Castle, about 6 miles to the north of Whitchurch.

Parking: There is a car park at the side of the inn. Alternatively, there are parking facilities within the grounds of Cholmondeley Castle.

Length of the walk: Within the park and gardens of Cholmondeley Castle you will probably cover about 3 miles. The separate walk, which is recommended for those times when the park and gardens are closed, is 5 miles. Map: OS Landranger 117 Chester (inn GR 553505).

Here is an opportunity to meander along some of Cheshire's quiet lanes and cross rich agricultural land via paths and tracks in a very scenic part of the country.

When the park and gardens of Cholmondeley Castle Estate are open, you will probably be content just to stroll through the lovely parkland setting, where there are lakes, woodlands and beautiful gardens to admire.

The park and gardens are open on Sunday and bank holiday afternoons during April, and on Wednesday, Thursday, Sunday and bank holiday afternoons between May and the beginning of October. For information, telephone: 01829 720383.

The Walk

On leaving the inn, turn right and cross the busy A49 road to enter Bickerton Road. Keep forward, ignoring a turn off to the right (which is the route to Cholmondeley Castle Park and Gardens) and, after 1 mile, turn left to enter a lane where a sign points towards 'Bickley'. Keep on past the entrance of Crosslanes Farm and then continue over a crossing lane. At the next junction, turn left in the direction of Bickley. After Pipehouse Farm, the way is next left, to enter a narrow lane which commences at the side of the precincts of St Wenefrede's church, Bickley.

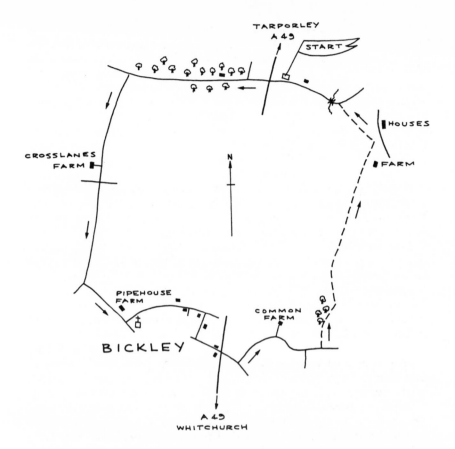

The church is of strong appearance, being constructed of sandstone blocks under a tiled roof. Internally, the most attractive feature is the timber passage aisle on the north side. There is a fine hammerbeam roof.

Continue along the narrow lane which takes you away from the church. Pass Cholmondeley Coronation Hall and St Wenefrede's Green to arrive at a junction of lanes by a dwelling called Woodfield. Turn right here, pass Moss Cottage, then turn left at the T-junction in the direction of Wrenbury and Nantwich. Cross the busy A49 road and, after a further 250 metres, turn left, again in the direction of Wrenbury and Nantwich. After ¼ mile, pass the entrance drive of Common Farm and, 300 metres further on, pass a narrow lane which goes off to the right. About 150 metres after passing this lane, keep an eye open for a footpath which commences through a field gate on the left, where a sign indicates 'Chorley'.

Go through the gate, cross the field and pass through a facing gate at the field corner. Pass over a stream via wide wooden plank-bridges and follow a grassy track, with a wood on the left. A straight 200 metres takes you to a gate which gives access to a large field. Cross the field, bearing left, and go through a gate near the field corner.

Keep along the left-hand edge of the next three fields, passing through a gate and going over a stile en route. At the end of the third field go over a fence-stile in a facing hedgerow. Cross the next field in the direction of dwellings which can be seen about 400 metres away and, after about 100 metres, go over a stile in a crossing hedgerow. This stile is set between two large trees. Continue in the general direction of the dwellings, aiming slightly to their right, to go over a bridge which carries a track over a dyke.

On crossing the bridge turn left and walk along the edge of a rough field, keeping the dyke and a hedgerow on your immediate left. Continue to the field corner, where a stile gives access to a crossing lane. Turn left along the lane, go over a bridge and, after a further 300 metres, arrive back at the Cholmondeley Arms and the car.

The Alternative Walk

On leaving the inn, turn right and cross the busy A49 road to enter Bickerton Road. Turn next right, to follow a lane which quickly turns to the left and leads to the entrance pay kiosk of Cholmondeley Castle Park and Gardens. The castle itself is a private dwelling and as such, access is unavailable.

Immediately on passing the pay kiosk there is a junction of ways. A facing drive goes straight ahead over a cattle grid, but turn left, pass a private drive on the right which leads to a dwelling, then go through a facing gateway to follow a rough macadam drive, which turns to the right. Pass through a gate at the side of a cattle grid, walk past Deer Park Lodge and continue along the tree-lined drive.

After $1/4$ mile, pass over a bridge between two lakes and bear right, away from the drive, to walk in the direction of the castle, which can be seen $1/4$ mile away on higher ground. Over to the right there is a cricket ground. Arrive at a car park which is in front of a ha-ha (sandstone wall and fence) on the lower ground below the castle.

Enter the castle gardens by the small Badminton Gate, which leads off the car park. (This is where the map and guide booklet come into their own.) It should be noted at this point that the following described route through the gardens is only an optional one and visitors are at liberty to walk where they please, provided they keep to designated public paths.

Climb forward to where there is a crossing path, halfway up the slope. Turn right to follow this path, go under a Spanish chestnut tree and

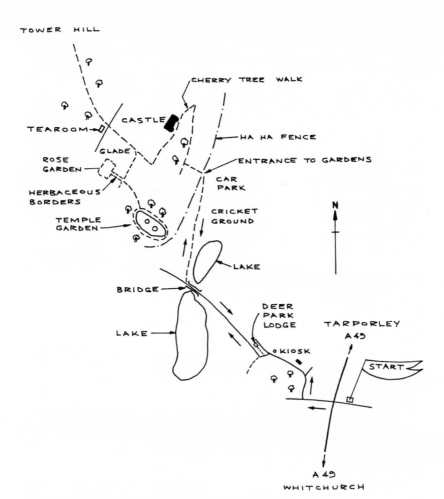

The alternative walk.

then turn sharp left to ascend the Cherry Tree Walk, which takes you between the overhanging branches of Japanese cherry trees. At the top of the ascent, turn left and follow a grassy track, which keeps to the terrace wall. Pass by steps leading up to the castle terrace and walk forward (unless you wish for a quick detour to the gift shop on the right), to descend and arrive at a crossing gravel track. Turn right and follow this path to the Glade – which is dominated by a 30 year old magnolia.

Close by is the Rose Garden, which is entered via an archway in a surrounding hedge. From the Rose Garden the route is via the

The castle and parkland at Cholmondeley.

Herbaceous Borders, along a gravel path, to enter the Temple Garden through a stone gatehouse.

The Temple Garden is a delightful place through which to meander – the main feature being a small lake with two, bridged, islands. On one of the islands there is a temple – from which the garden takes its name. The lake is stocked with Koi carp and is surrounded by numerous waterside plants, which provide a delightful vista throughout spring, summer and autumn.

Having sampled the delights of the Temple Garden, it might be a good idea at this point to take some light refreshment at the tearoom. Therefore, retrace your route back to the Glade and follow a path on the left which takes you straight there.

Having rested for a while, you may wish to ascend Tower Hill, the path to which commences at the side of the tearoom. Climb and take a right-hand fork to ascend through woods. The path eventually takes you clear of the trees, where there are long views to enjoy over the gardens and surrounding parkland before descending back to the tearoom.

On the conclusion of your meanderings through the gardens, make your way back to the car park at the bottom of the slope. From here, walk back to the bridge between the two lakes and retrace your initial route back to the Cholmondeley Arms and the car.

20 Aston
The Bhurtpore Inn

Not far from Nantwich, the village of Aston is situated in the rich farming country of south Cheshire. There are many old farmhouses in the area, together with a large mill and an interesting pottery.

The pub has a very unusual name. Bhurtpore is a fortified city in India which was captured by British troops during 1826. The troops were under the command of Viscount Combermere, of nearby Combermere Abbey, on whose estate the pub then stood – hence, an Indian name in the heart of Cheshire! The theme has been continued by the present owners, who are well known for their tasty home-made curries and balti dishes. There are Indian mementoes, photographs and pottery to be seen inside – although, glancing through the available choices of food and drink, it soon becomes apparent that here is a most cosmopolitan hostelry indeed.

The selection of drinks is quite amazing. There are around 60 malt whiskies and over 120 (and growing) specialist bottled beers. Hanby Drawwell Bitter, brewed in Wem, and up to nine other guest beers can also be sampled. There is a guest cider and a guest Belgian ale, together with Bitburger Pils, an unpasteurised German lager, to further extend the offerings.

The menu, which is complemented by a daily specials board, is varied and keenly priced. Among the starters are mushrooms in cream, tiger prawns in filo pastry, crispy-coated vegetables and prawn cocktail. The main courses, apart from the curries, include home-cooked ham, pan-fried pork fillet, lamb chops, gammon, steak, kidney and real ale pie, chicken breast, braised steak, battered whole tail scampi, fresh salmon fillet and various steaks. There is a selection of vegetarian main courses, and snacks and light meals can also be purchased. The desserts on offer include various flavours of ice cream, apple pie, lemon brûlée, sticky toffee pudding and chocolate fudge cake. The children are not forgotten, for they have their own menu from which to choose. They are welcome to eat inside, if accompanied, but the landlord requests that they do not stay too late into the evening. The inn has a beer garden and children's play area outside.

Food is served every day between 12 noon and 2 pm and during the evening between 7 pm and 9 pm.

Telephone: 01270 780917.

How to get there: The A530 connects Nantwich with Whitchurch. The village of Aston, which is about 5 miles from Nantwich, straddles this road. From the A530 enter Wrenbury Road, pass St Andrew's Methodist church and arrive at the Bhurtpore Inn, which is on the left.

Parking: There is a large car park at the side of the inn. There is also a small car park at the Firs Pottery – but this is specifically for visitors to the pottery, and should not be used by those who wish to carry out the walk.

Length of the walk: 2½ miles. Map: OS Landranger 118 Stoke-on-Trent and Macclesfield (inn GR 690471).

A short, but varied, route, initially along field paths and then by tracks and lanes through the rich farming country of south Cheshire – coupled with a visit to a pottery, where you can observe, and even take part in, the pottery making process – makes for a very interesting ramble.

The Walk

On leaving the front door of the inn, turn left and follow the lane past Newhall Cross House and other dwellings. About 30 metres before the lane turns sharply to the left, go over a stile on the right, which is at the side of a field gate. Walk forward and pass through a gap in a crossing fence, then bear slightly right, to go over a stile at the field corner.

Follow the next field edge, keeping a fence, hedge and trees, on your immediate right. Cross a stile at the field corner, and continue, but after

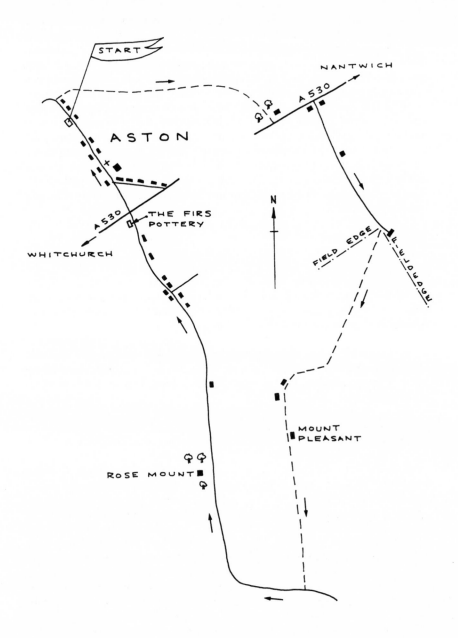

START

ASTON

NANTWICH

A 530

A 530

WHITCHURCH

THE FIRS
POTTERY

N

FIELD EDGE

FIELD EDGE

MOUNT
PLEASANT

ROSE MOUNT

only 40 metres, go over another stile and follow the edge of a large field, where the hedge is now on your immediate left. A stile at the field corner takes you into another field. Continue along the field edge in the direction of buildings which can be seen straight ahead. At the field corner a stile gives access to a facing hedged-in track. After 60 metres pass through a gate and continue to a crossing road.

Turn left and follow the roadside, but after only 120 metres and opposite a dwelling called Sandford Cottage, turn right to enter a rough, narrow lane. After 200 metres walk past a small farm and continue to where, after a further 150 metres, there is a facing gate and entrance drive to a dwelling. Do not go through this gate but pass over a stile on the right, at the side of a field gate. You have now entered a very large field where navigational care is required in order to follow the path which crosses over it.

With the stile at your back, walk diagonally left, bisecting the field edges, which go off to left and right. On reaching the far side of the field go over a stile and turn right to follow a field edge. After 120 metres pass over a double stile and plank-bridge to enter a narrow, rough field – where a dwelling can be seen about 200 metres away on slightly higher ground, straight ahead. Walk forward, and after a further 60 metres go over a stile and plank-bridge. Keep on, across rough ground, keeping a hedgerow on your immediate right, and after 60 metres turn left and pass over a plank-bridge. Pass to the left of an outbuilding, to continue, keeping a fence and the dwelling on your right. Go over a stile, which is set in the fence on your right, to enter the approach drive to the dwelling you have just walked past. Turn left, away from the dwelling, and go through a gate.

Pass a dwelling called Mount Pleasant and continue along a rough, gravel track. Emerge from the track at a crossing lane, where the way is right. Keep on past a dwelling called Rose Mount and follow the lane into the outskirts of the village of Aston. Pass Sheppenhall Grove, which goes off to the right, and continue past a mixture of dwellings to arrive at the Firs Pottery, which is on the left, just before a crossing road is reached.

The Pottery makes a vast range of functional and decorative pots using stoneware clay which is fired at 1260°C in electric and gas kilns. A showroom is attached. Visitors can also spend time actually making their own pottery. Apart from the Pottery, there is a very attractive garden area that visitors are allowed to enjoy, and it is a very pleasant spot in which to relax for a while. Telephone for information: 01270 780345.

On leaving the Firs Pottery go over the crossing road to enter the facing Wrenbury Road, then keep straight ahead, to arrive back at the Bhurtpore Inn and the car.